G000136897

BECKETT
BEFORE BECKETT

Also by Brigitte Le Juez

Irlande, with Agnès Maillot (Larousse, 1989)

Modern French Short Fiction, co-edited with Johnnie Gratton
(Manchester University Press, 1994)

Le Papegai et le Papelard dans 'Un Coeur Simple'
de Gustave Flaubert (Rodopi, 1999)

Clergés et Cultures Populaires (Publications
de l'Université de Saint-Etienne, 2004)

BECKETT
BEFORE BECKETT

BRIGITTE LE JUEZ

Translated by Ros Schwartz

Souvenir Press

First published in Great Britain in 2008 by Souvenir Press Ltd
43 Great Russell Street, London WC1B 3PD

This paperback edition 2009

First published in France in 2007 by Editions Grasset & Fasquelle
under the title *Beckett avant la lettre*

English translation © Souvenir Press and Ros Schwartz

The right of Brigitte Le Juez to be identified as the author
of this work has been asserted by her in accordance with the
Copyright, Designs and Patents Act, 1988

All rights reserved. No part of this publication may
be reproduced, stored in a retrieval system or transmitted, in any form
or by any means, electronic, mechanical, photocopying, or otherwise,
without the prior permission of the Copyright owner.

ISBN 9780285638624

Typeset by M Rules

ACKNOWLEDGEMENTS

I would like to express my warmest gratitude to all those who helped me complete this book: Edward Beckett, executor of the Samuel Beckett Estate; Rachel Burrows' family who gave me permission, through Trinity College Library, Dublin, to use the manuscript of her student notebook; Trinity College Library, in particular Jane Maxwell, librarian in the Manuscripts department, who handles the rights for this manuscript and who advised and assisted me in my work; the Bibliothèque Nationale de France, for allowing me access to all the necessary documents; my university, Dublin City University, and especially my department, The School of Applied Language and Intercultural Studies, for having granted me a sabbatical; and lastly, to my husband, Brian Duffy, who has always shared my admiration for Samuel Beckett, for his constant support.

ACKNOWLEDGMENTS

For my parents

CONTENTS

"ENSEIGNER, C'EST S'EXHIBER."[1]

About twelve years ago, in the course of my research for a thesis on how Gustave Flaubert's work was received in Ireland, I was looking for evidence that would enable me to state with certainty that Samuel Beckett had read Flaubert. I had no doubt that this was the case. Other scholars had already made this assumption, but without any factual basis. Unlike Oscar Wilde or James Joyce, among the most illustrious of his compatriots known to have been influenced by Flaubert, Beckett had never mentioned his admiration for the great master. A few clues scattered here and there in his work pointed to an affinity that had still to be confirmed. As I conducted my research in the Old Library of Trinity College, Dublin, I happened upon a notebook that had belonged to one of Beckett's students when he taught French literature there, from 1930 to 1931. Like a hidden treasure, this document could only be reached at the end of a maze of corridors and staircases crossing the Long Room, where the famous *Book of Kells*, the illuminated manuscript dating back to 800, is kept (access to this room has since been made easier, and

1

there is even a lift). This manuscript gave me new insight into Beckett. It revealed not only Beckett the admirer of Flaubert whom I had desperately been seeking, but also a Beckett with very definite opinions on French literature, a Beckett who would never reveal himself in this manner again during his lifetime.

This notebook is relatively little known since it can only be consulted in the manuscript room of Trinity College Library. But that does not explain why it has remained unpublished and untranslated. Those researchers who have consulted it have made little use of it. And yet, these notes which Beckett's student, Rachel Burrows (née Dobbin), bequeathed to her university in 1977, have attracted the interest of leading Beckett scholars, including Stanley Gontarski, professor at Florida State University, who, with two colleagues, interviewed Ms Burrows in 1982. This interview provides a unique commentary on the notebook since Ms Burrows adds a few affectionate memories of her former lecturer. However, she sheds little new light on what she wrote some fifty years earlier. Perhaps this explains why potential publishers of the manuscript have lost heart, particularly as it does not contain the writings of Beckett himself, and the document is not easy to read. These notes were scribbled in a little notebook seventy-five years ago, and, like all notes, were sometimes written at great speed and are in places difficult to make out. And there is an additional complication: the original, which initially I had looked at, has been mislaid. For the time being, the notebook is only available on microfilm.

All the same, though it is not a text by Beckett, and though it is hard to decipher, this little notebook deserves to reach a wider readership, not only because it represents a unique record of Beckett's teaching of French literature, but also, and above all, because it affords a glimpse into Beckett's very personal view of literature, some precepts of which appear later in his writing. His choices of lecture material reveal his own preferences, where he situated himself in literature, signalling the path he would take after his brief spell as a lecturer.

Rachel Burrows took notes mainly in English, with quotations in French. It is hard to tell whether Beckett taught in English or French, or a mixture of the two. Ms Burrows sometimes gives the impression that she was translating. Her notes are written in somewhat quirky English and the French quotations contain a number of errors. In the interests of clarity, I have corrected the various mistakes the student made on encountering the language of literary criticism for the first time – she was only nineteen years old. And I have paraphrased or added the odd syntactical element in square brackets to make clearer the sections that are too disjointed and convey the full thrust of Beckett's arguments.

The aim of Beckett's course was to introduce his students to modern literature. The choice of set books, Gide for the novel and Racine for drama, may seem surprising. Gide was of course a contemporary author but Racine belonged to the classical canon. Was Beckett playing with the very notion of modernity? The content of his lectures does not suggest this. How was it that he was given this freedom of choice in a conventional institution? It turns out that the head of the French department at Trinity, Thomas Rudmose-Brown, was something of an eccentric. He had taught Beckett, and had tremendous respect for him, trusting him to teach works that would interest the younger generation. Beckett was twenty-five years old.

The course begins with an introduction to the novel. The young lecturer takes into account the other classes his students have attended. They are mentioned at the end of the manuscript:

3

"Hugo, Vigny: Wednesday", "Balzac: Thursday", for example. His intention, therefore, is to revisit 19th-century French literature, to make the connection with contemporary authors. And modernity, which is very much on the agenda, also applies to Racine, whose originality and contemporaneousness he will demonstrate when he moves on to the theatre.

In principle, the course's structure, as manifested in the notebook, is very clear: Introduction (reflections on literature), Part 1: The novel (Gide), Part 2: Drama (Racine), Conclusion (return to the novel and the notion of modernity). That said, like any good course, it includes a lot of repetition. In order to be sure that his students have thoroughly absorbed the fundamental notions they need to acquire, Beckett, who is a conscientious teacher, often returns to the same ideas, developing different aspects and drawing on different examples. For the sake of clarity, I have grouped the various topics together but I have kept to the original structure, beginning with Beckett's reflections on the works of Balzac and Proust before he moves on to Gide and then Racine, the main components of the course.

Beckett was in fact marking time at Trinity College and already knew he was not cut out for teaching. Some of his lectures were the fruit of his own reading and thinking which he had already published or hoped to publish in future, a future he had difficulty envisaging. Although a reluctant teacher, he was a painstaking one and tried to show his students how to tell a good work from a bad one by comparing authors whose conceptions of literature were diametrically opposed.

What we discover thanks to this notebook is a new facet of this brief period in Samuel Beckett's life, before he wrote his first novel, *Dream of Fair to Middling Women*, which did not meet with success, failing even to find a publisher, and which Beckett gave up on and wished to forget. It was published only posthumously and in English.

This notebook, which the far-sighted Rachel Burrows had carefully kept for all those years, sheds light on a shadowy period in the development of one of the greatest writers of our time and allows us to discover Beckett before Beckett.

BECKETT AND
FRENCH LITERATURE

PORTRAIT OF THE ARTIST
AS A YOUNG STUDENT

Born into a prosperous Dublin Protestant family, Samuel Beckett learned French at an early age, at a private primary school. Between the ages of eight and thirteen, he attended a bilingual school run by a Frenchman, Alfred Le Peton. Middle-class families such as Beckett's considered learning French to be a refinement. However, we can hardly surmise that this period of his education stimulated his interest in France. Mr Le Peton was a very strict teacher and, according to some, not a very good one. But the boys liked him, especially as he instilled in them a spirit of tolerance which made a lasting impression on Beckett. The pupils were not all of the same faith, and Le Peton insisted that they accept each other. Beckett spent his secondary school years as a boarder at Portora Royal School (like Oscar Wilde before him), a chiefly Protestant establishment, located in Enniskillen, Northern Ireland, where he continued to study French without distinguishing himself particularly. On the other hand, reading was already one of his favourite pastimes. At home, his family read few literary works. His father was particularly fond of popular novels while his mother read only the newspaper, occasionally, and the Bible, every day, especially to her children. Before going away to boarding school at the age of nine, Beckett had set up his own little library in a corner of his room where he installed a bust of Shakespeare – beside which he later added a bust of Dante. He did not really begin to show an interest in French literature until his arrival at Trinity College at the age of seventeen.

It is common knowledge that during his years as a *lecteur* (teaching assistant) in Paris, he was influenced by Joyce, particularly as he had helped him with the early drafts of *Finnegans Wake*. According to James Knowlson, Beckett's official biographer: "Discussion of his formative influences has tended to concentrate on Joyce or Dante. Yet, although both were vitally important to him, it was also his good fortune [. . .] to have Racine (for the drama) and Diderot as well as Stendhal (for the novel) as his forerunners. Nor did he object to being placed in the company of Rabelais . . .".[2] In Trinity College library there are notes on *Gargantua* and *Pantagruel* that had belonged to Beckett. Some of the humorous, sometimes scatological references which he had copied from the two books bring to mind certain characters that appear later in his own writing.[3]

His love of literature led him straight to university and later into teaching. It was as a student and afterwards as a junior lecturer at Trinity College that Beckett acquired his knowledge of the authors discussed here.

According to *The Dublin University Calendar*, the undergraduate French literature programme comprised works from the Middle Ages, the 16th century (Ronsard, Scève), the 17th (Molière, Corneille and Racine), the 18th (Marivaux), the 19th (Balzac, Huysmans and Stendhal) and the 20th (including Proust and Gide). During his final year, Beckett discovered the poetry of

Pierre Jean Jouve and Jules Romains, and developed a particular interest in Unanimism. In 1989, he told James Knowlson that he had cultivated a real passion for Jouve's pre-World War I poems.

Lois Gordon maintains that the economic situation in Ireland at the time Beckett entered Trinity College, in 1923 – in other words after World War I and Irish independence –, was significant. An eyewitness to scenes of national uprising (when he was only ten years old his father took him to see Dublin in flames), and an avid reader, Beckett would have been aware of the debates and works by contemporary authors probing the relationship between morality and nationalism. The religious question, which was central to this discussion, remained a thorny issue in Ireland for a long time. Not only did religious and political allegiances often overlap, but they also reflected class divisions. Beckett, a product of the Protestant class which tended to be pro-British and middle-class, must have been conscious of this, as he was someone who already had, and always would have, friends from varied backgrounds.

What haunted him from this period was the memory of the devastation, death and injustice and, for some survivors, extreme poverty and despair. His own experience during World War II would certainly not alter his view of human suffering, of *"l'abîme"* (the abyss) which each of us must face. These considerations would make him receptive to certain authors like Dostoevsky and Gide, as we shall see later.

According to James Knowlson, Thomas Rudmose-Brown, the professor of Romance languages at Trinity College, took an interest in Beckett from the very start: "Even in his first Junior Freshman year, Beckett's aptitude for French and English literature, his thoughtful appreciation of the texts that they were studying and his unusual essays, as well as his silent, brooding manner, brought him to the Professor's notice. Much later, Beckett acknowledged that Rudmose-Brown 'opened all kind of doors for me'."[4] These doors were varied: not only did Rudmose-Brown encourage Beckett in his literary explorations, but he also advised him to go on his first trip to France and gave him his first teaching jobs in France and Ireland where, again thanks to Rudmose-Brown, an academic career was open to him.

As regards literary discoveries, alongside the classical authors, Rudmose-Brown – "Ruddy" as his students and colleagues nicknamed him affectionately (or otherwise) – liked to include in the curriculum contemporary writers, most of whom his Irish colleagues were barely acquainted with. When it came to drama, he was a Racine scholar and he passed on his knowledge and enthusiasm for the playwright to his young protégé.

Rudmose-Brown's love of poetry was infectious, and it was he who introduced Beckett to Louise Labé[5] and Pierre de Ronsard (particularly the *Sonnets pour Hélène [Sonnets to Helen]*). In 1926 and 1927, he included 19th-century poets on the syllabus (Paul Verlaine, José Maria de Heredia, Leconte de Lisle) as well as modern poets (Henri de Régnier, Valery Larbaud, Francis Jammes, Léon-Paul Fargue and Paul Valéry – Beckett would subsequently meet the latter two in Paris). And as for the novel, in his final year, Beckett studied Proust (*Du côté de chez Swann [Swann's Way]*) and Gide (*Isabelle* and *La Porte étroite [Strait is the Gate]*).

This combination of knowledge of the classics and curiosity for the authors of the time that Rudmose-Brown transmitted to his students is echoed in the course Beckett taught in 1930–31, on his return from Paris, after his stint as a *lecteur* at the École Normale Supérieure de Paris. It should be added that in the eyes of his colleagues, Ruddy was an independent, nonconformist

12

character (he was anticlerical in an Ireland that was strongly influenced by religion), whom Beckett described as a "free spirit".[6] Ruddy in turn described Beckett as a *"libre penseur"* (free thinker) in the letter he sent to Valery Larbaud: "One of my brightest students, an enemy of imperialism, patriotism and all the Churches, Sam Beckett, is currently at the École Normal(e) Supérieure, 45 rue d'Ulm, as an English *lecteur*. He is very keen to make your acquaintance".[7]

In August 1926, having decided to go to France to improve his spoken French, Beckett set off on a meticulously planned bicycle tour of Touraine and the châteaux of the Loire Valley. He took this opportunity to pay tribute to the region's great authors whom he had discovered in the course of his undergraduate studies: Ronsard (La Poissonnière, Vendôme and Saint-Côme-les-Tours), Rabelais (La Devinière and Chinon), Joachim du Bellay (*Le petit Liré*), Descartes (La Flèche), Alfred de Vigny (Loches) and Balzac (Tours, Saumur and Vendôme).[8] This trip, which he enjoyed enormously, was the first of a series of literary pilgrimages he made to France over the next decade.

On his return to Dublin, he met Alfred Péron, who had come over to Trinity from the École Normale as a French *lecteur*. Péron had shared an office with Jean-Paul Sartre and Paul Nizan at the École Normale. A refined and cultured young man, he was a valued friend to Beckett and a brilliant interlocutor. Péron became the driving force behind the Modern Languages Society which Beckett and his friends enthusiastically joined.

Beckett was an ardent reader, taking copious notes and using them as a basis for his own writing. From very early on he steeped himself in French writers and philosophers. For example he read Descartes avidly, filling three loose-leaf notebooks with his own thoughts and impressions, as well as with quotes from literary critics and biographies. For a fairly long period, Descartes was an important source of inspiration to him. His first published poem, *Whoroscope*, was written one night in June 1930, during his time in Paris. Beckett had penned it at the last minute for the sole purpose of entering a poetry competition, the prize being a sum of money and publication of the winning poem. He won. Immersed in the philosopher's writings, he found in Descartes the stimulus he needed to produce a hundred or so lines on the competition theme: Time. *Whoroscope* is a narration by Descartes himself, evoking his life, his work and his times. The poem is full of humour (it mentions the philosopher's fondness for eight-to-ten-day-old eggs) and some highly obscure allusions. It could be seen as a form of satire on the academics whose ranks Beckett was expected to join on his return to Dublin. Back at Trinity in November 1930, he drew on Descartes again to deliver a witty lecture entitled "Le Concentrisme", a non-existent theory on a made-up French poet, one Jean du Chas, ironically suicidal and author of a *Discours de la sortie* (Discourse on Exits).[9] Beckett had invented a complete biography of this Jean du Chas, loosely based on his own personal details (for example, he gave du Chas his own date of birth, 13 April 1906).[10] The subject led to a debate. It was said that some colleagues were taken in, that others even went so far as to claim that this so-called poet and his movement were not unknown to them, and that they were not amused when the whole thing was revealed as a hoax, but Beckett himself stated categorically that his audience knew exactly what he was up to.

At the beginning of his final undergraduate year at Trinity, in 1927, Beckett had already built up a reputation for having a brilliant and somewhat unorthodox mind. He achieved such excellent results in his finals that he was awarded the highest distinction in modern languages, as well as a (real) gold medal for modern literature and a grant of fifty pounds, a large sum of money at the time, for his outstanding dissertation on Descartes. In addition to these accolades, on the enthusiastic recommendation of Rudmose-Brown, he was given the post of English *lecteur* at the École Normale in rue d'Ulm. This position would allow him to study and teach there for two years (from 1928 to 1930) and on his return to obtain a teaching post at Trinity. During his stay in France, Beckett was supposed to write a thesis. He intended to do his research on Jouve, Romains and the Unanimists.

His academic career seemed all mapped out. Rudmose-Brown encouraged him. His parents were delighted, even though they could not understand how their son could be so different from the rest of the family. There was nothing eccentric about the Becketts' way of life. However, not only did their youngest son have no interest in the family business, but also, according to Deirdre Bair, one of Beckett's biographers, after his travels on the continent, he had begun to wear a French beret and to pepper his conversation with Gallicisms which his parents could not understand. Nonetheless, they recognised the prestige attached to an academic career and supported him in his choice.

Between receiving his degree and leaving for his two-year spell as a *lecteur* in France, Beckett needed to earn a living. Again thanks to Rudmose-Brown, he was offered a job in Belfast as a French teacher at a residential public school for boys. But this was not a happy experience and did not bode well for his future as a teacher.

On his arrival in Paris, Beckett had no inkling that his life was to change for ever. He was entering a world of intellectuals and poets which included Irish writers who had fled the moral and artistic constraints of their new country (the Irish Free State was born, but it was not yet entirely free). It was through them that he was to meet his already famous compatriot, James Joyce, among others.

It was also during his stay in France, and through his literary encounters, that Beckett began to write. An essay, "Dante . . . Bruno. Vico.. Joyce", and a short story, *Assumption*, were published in the prestigious journal *transition* in June 1929. But his first publication of note was *Proust*. Instead of embarking seriously on his thesis on Jouve and the Unanimists, which he was to describe in an interview with Lawrence Harvey as a "ridiculous essay", and to James Knowlson as a "scrappy work", Beckett preferred to take his first steps in the direction of literary creativity, throwing himself into an essay on Marcel Proust.

Jean-Michel Rabaté describes this essay as: "neither correspondence nor testimony, biography or literary criticism, the essay deliberately and immediately differentiates itself from the main trends of Proustian criticism of the time."[11] At twenty-four, Beckett had burgeoned into a brilliant independent thinker and his essay was extremely well received by English critics.

According to Deirdre Bair, the essay on Proust "shows how much Proust influenced Beckett and is probably his first attempt to formulate a literary credo of his own. The essay reveals Beckett's literary conscience in its formative phase."[12] This monograph, devoted to *A la recherche du temps perdu [Remembrance of Things Past]*, draws parallels between Proust's work and that of Joyce. "Here form is content, content is form. [. . .] His writing is not *about* something; *it is that something itself*,"[13] wrote Beckett on *Work in Progress* (which was to become *Finnegans Wake*). Similarly, Beckett considered that, for Proust, form was inseparable from content. He would return to that idea during his teaching.

What Beckett seems to admire most in Proust, and which is of significance for what is to follow (in particular his criticism of

Balzac), is his antipathy towards superficial modes of uniformity and coherence. For Beckett, literature offers two challenges: that of formulating a reality stripped to its essence rather than one concerned with events, and that of acknowledging life's complexity and reflecting it fully, in particular its astounding *"principe de désintégration"* (principle of disintegration) – *"parfaitement intelligible et parfaitement inexplicable"* [perfectly intelligible and perfectly inexplicable] were the words he used to present the work of his imaginary poet –, it is a principle that recurs in Beckett from the very early days.

Just like the principles stated during his lectures on the set texts, and we will return to this later, those found in *Proust* say a lot more about Beckett than they do about the author of *A la Recherche du temps perdu*. That in any case is the view of some critics who see in it insightful and original ideas, but primarily an opportunity for Beckett to diagnose his own problems – as Beckett himself confirms: "[the book is] at its best a distorted steam-rolled equivalent of some aspects or confusion of aspects in myself."[14] As his correspondence with his friend Thomas MacGreevy in 1930 reveals, the writing of *Proust* was a hard slog, and when the book was finally published, Beckett, already back in Ireland, could only see its flaws.

The completion of his work on *Proust* marked the end of his stay in Paris and the beginning of the academic career he did not want, but which he took up for lack of any alternative. He was deeply dissatisfied at the time he started his three-year contract with Trinity College. As it turned out, he barely managed to complete half that time.

BECKETT AS TEACHER

The dissertation on Jouve, Romains and the Unanimists, which Beckett had undertaken to write on his departure from Dublin, was hastily produced during the summer of 1928 – and was never actually submitted (and, moreover, has disappeared) – as Beckett devoted his time and energy to assisting Joyce and working on his Proust essay. His tutors at Trinity were disappointed but agreed to take into consideration his Paris publications (in particular *Proust*) and he was awarded his Master's degree. After the agreed three years as a lecturer, the young man could expect a permanent appointment making him a fully-fledged academic.

But that was to ignore the fact that Beckett loathed teaching and felt awkward taking classes made up of mainly female students. Some of his former students had vivid memories of the young junior lecturer. They were immediately mesmerised by him. Aileen Conan, for example, recalls: "A very handsome young man. We were thrilled with him the first time we walked into his class. Very handsome indeed he was, but he had a distracted look, his blue eyes trying to avoid us – as if to say 'well I have this bunch in front of me now, I must try and do something for them.' Not in an unkind way, because one felt that he was – 'shy' might be the word for it. He faced us all with a distracted air, or abstracted might be the better word. But one felt he didn't enjoy lecturing. He didn't seem to be very good, nor did he want to be, at communicating. I think he just felt that he was going to give us what he felt about these poets and writers and didn't want to worry about it otherwise. At that time we were not aware that he had written anything but we did think he was brilliant."[15]

Rachel Burrows draws a warm and enthusiastic portrait: "I had gone to Paris in the summer of 1931 [. . .].Then I came back to find that a Mister Beckett was our junior French lecturer for 'Racine and the Modern Novel.' We knew nothing about him. [. . .] none of us could foresee that our tall, taciturn, rather self-effacing young lecturer was going to revolutionize the form of European theatre. I don't believe any of our year knew him well, except perhaps Leslie O'Daikin, who wrote to me shortly before he died saying, 'Sam is in London. We are having great fun.' Seems an odd word to use in connection with Sam Beckett. He seldom smiled. [. . .] I remember him in his long dark overcoat, collar turned up, thick hair standing stiffly *'en brosse'*. His pale blue eyes fixed you with complete attention and yet with a strange remote quality. [. . .] He was a very impersonal lecturer. He said what he had to say and then left the lecture room. But he was very courteous and always willing to elucidate a point, if anyone had the courage to ask him a question. I believe he considered himself a bad lecturer and that makes me sad because he was so good. [. . .] Many of his students would, unfortunately, agree with him, and they made little effort to try and understand him. [. . .] This may have been why we so seldom saw the genial side of his personality. He probably felt that we were as bored with him as he was with us. In my case, it was far from the truth. Looking back, I'm glad, as young as I was, I was just nineteen, I was aware that here was a brilliant mind. Here was exciting material that could not be found in a book, and I made it my business to take down his lectures as fully as possible."[16]

As for his teaching style, she concedes that he had an usual way of going about it: "He would make long pauses between phrases, or very often pause in the wrong place, after a word which might make you lose the thread of his thought. [. . .] In lecturing, some people like Beckett, are creating as they go along. Suddenly he would come up with something better than what he'd been going to say."

Rachel Burrows' admiration for her former lecturer enabled her to see this episode in Beckett's life in a positive light. His own feelings were very different. In a letter to Deirdre Bair, Beckett confirms that he did not like having in front of him all these young women "mooning about": "I was sorely tempted to ask them all to get out, to leave the room".[17] According to his friends, his distaste for the idea of having to stand in front of an audience of giggling girls provided him an excuse to drink excessively on the eve of his lectures so as to forget momentarily what awaited him the next day. In front of his students, however, he gave the best of himself.

THE NOVEL

BALZAC, STENDHAL, FLAUBERT, PROUST

Before moving on to what Beckett taught his students about Gide and Racine, based on Rachel Burrows' notes, it is essential to underline his position on Balzac. Beckett effectively used him as a counter-example in his literary analyses and in his reflections on modern literature and realism. Of course, Beckett was not the only one of his generation to adopt this position, but Balzac's detractors tended to be in France, not in Ireland. Balzac was on the Trinity College degree syllabus (alternatively *Eugénie Grandet*, *Ursule Mirouët* and *La Cousine Bette*). Beckett had therefore discovered him early on, at a time when Balzac was much loved by Irish readers, unlike Flaubert. In an article written in 1946 entitled *"The Irish Conscience?"*, Seán O'Faoláin, editor of the literary review *The Bell*, partially explains why. French authors had a great deal of influence on the writers of his generation, in particular Balzac (and this phenomenon had begun in the second half of the 19th century). "Is it significant that when Irish writers are asked what authors have influenced them they rarely mention Flaubert?" he asks, and continues: "Their natural bent, their tradition as inheritors of a literary movement which was wholly a romantic movement, is towards the imagination. Birth and upbringing, the political events of three generations, historical loyalties, all draw them back to common life. We can no more escape the peasant, whom we often loathe [. . .] nor the bourgeois of our time [. . .] than Flaubert could – or did. We should surely, then, feel a considerable sympathy for Flaubert, torn likewise between the delights of the imagination and the aggravations of a crude society? Our loss of sympathy with Flaubert, I feel, starts when we discover the force of his central creed – impersonality. [. . .] Balzac's realism is his realism, a broad connotation. Flaubert's is restricted, concentrated, detailed, particular, limited, too much of a literary gospel. We bow down before *Madame Bovary*: we prefer the wider scope of Balzac."

The differences between Balzac and Flaubert fascinated some Irish writers, like George Moore whose preference for Balzac was determined by Flaubert's impersonality. Moore claimed that "if Balzac had written *Madame Bovary*, he would have written it better; he would have given it bigger lungs and a faster beating heart. The characters would be open like a flowing river."[18] In her study of Flaubert's reception in England (and it is significant because most of the literary reviews available in Ireland up until the 20th century were English), Mary Neale explains English writers' reticence towards Flaubertian style and suggests: "they will never completely adapt to French realism because of the nature itself of the English temperament; there will always be a certain desire for Romanticism, with the idealism it involves, to give a ray of hope in a life of disappointments, a desire which the Russian realist novel tends better to satisfy. The English have difficulty accepting a world governed by evil and total desolation."[19] But desolation is precisely Flaubert's territory, as George Sand's famous letter to Flaubert of 18 December 1875 confirms:

"Then you are going to start grubbing again? So am I; [. . .] What's our next move? For you, of course, desolation, and, for me, consolation. I do not know on what our destinies depend; you see them pass, you criticise them, you abstain from a literary appreciation of them, you limit yourself to depicting them, with deliberate meticulous concealment of your personal feelings. However, one sees them very clearly through your narrative, and you make the people sadder who read you. As for me, I should like to make them less sad."[20]

Beckett had a marked preference for Flaubert's style and subject matter. More specifically, it is the impersonality of Flaubert's writing that interested him, what O'Faoláin describes as the demarcation line that set him apart from most of their fellow writers. And consequently, that is what sets Beckett apart from his contemporaries. His lectures leave no doubt as to Flaubert's importance in his eyes: "Stendhal + Flaubert – real ancestors of modern novel, not Balzac", (95)[21] wrote Rachel Burrows in her notebook. From the first lecture, Beckett spoke of them in positive terms: "Both could be called realists. Background of Naturalistic novel – but authentic complexity lacking in Naturalists as in Romanticists. *Madame Bovary*, *Salammbô*: 2 different Flauberts. Not photographer or image monger". (3) The "authentic complexity", underlined in Rachel Burrows' notes, is a recurrent criterion in Beckett's literary judgments.

The importance of Stendhal and Flaubert had already been pointed out by Ezra Pound, the renowned American poet who was a Francophile and a friend of Joyce, and whom Beckett had met in Paris. In an essay entitled "*Dubliners* and Mr James Joyce", Pound writes: "There is a school of prose writers, and of verse writers for that matter, whose forerunner was Stendhal and whose founder was Flaubert. The followers of Flaubert deal in exact presentation. [. . .] They are perhaps the most clarifying and they have been perhaps the most beneficial force in modern writing."[22]

Beckett too, in citing Stendhal and Flaubert, implicitly aligns himself with the modern writers, distancing himself from his Irish contemporaries. Opposing that view, he adds with a disapproval which he passes on to his students: "In Balzac all reality is a determined, statistical entity, distorted, with total reality not respected." (21) This notion would be expanded in his own writing, from his first novel, *Dream of Fair to Middling Women*: "To read Balzac is to receive the impression of a chloroformed world. He is absolute master of his material, he can do what he likes with it, he can foresee and calculate its least vicissitude, he can write the end of his book before he has finished the first paragraph, because he has turned all his creatures into clockwork cabbages and can rely on their staying put wherever needed or staying going at whatever speed in whatever direction he chooses. The whole thing, from beginning to end, takes place in a spellbound backwash. We all love and lick up Balzac, we lap it up and say it is wonderful, but why call it a distillation of Euclid and Perrault *Scenes from life*? Why *human* comedy?"[23] With these words, Beckett shows to what extent, like Flaubert, he values the impersonality of the author and, above all, the absence of purpose in the text, the only possible conditions for the writer who wants specifically to try and express the human condition. There is no doubt that Beckett relished Flaubert's gibes at Balzac in *Bouvard et Pécuchet* [*Bouvard and Pécuchet*]:

"Balzac's work filled them with wonder, being at once like a teeming Babylon and specks of dust under the microscope [. . .]

'What an observer!' cried Bouvard.

'Personally I find him fanciful,' Pécuchet finally said. 'He believes in occult sciences, the monarch, the nobility, is dazzled by scoundrels, shoves millions around like centimes, and his bourgeois are not bourgeois, but supermen. Why inflate something that is flat and describe so many idiotic things! He writes one novel about chemistry, another about banking, another on printing machines [. . .]. We'll have one on every trade and every province, then on every town and every floor of every house, and every individual, and it will not be literature, but statistics or ethnography'."[24]

When he does read a novel by Balzac, Beckett too is astounded. On the subject of *La Cousine Bette*, he wrote to Thomas MacGreevy: "The bathos of style and thought is so enormous that I wonder is he writing seriously or in parody."[25] He also called Balzac the "Stock Exchange Hugo".[26]

Even in his book reviews for various newspapers, work which helped him make ends meet in his early days, Beckett only mentions Balzac better to discredit the authors in question. In June 1934, for example, for the *Spectator*, he wrote a critique of *Comment Proust a composé son roman* by Albert Feuillerat, attacking the author for desiring "the vulgarities of a plausible concatenation" and attempting to apply to Proust "the sweet reasonableness of plane psychology *à la Balzac* [. . .] the narrative trajectory that is more like a respectable parabola and less like the chart of an ague."[27]

Knowlson recalls that "it was his [Beckett's] good fortune to study Balzac – mostly so that he could reject his entire approach as a novelist", while on the subject of *Mercier et Camier*, he notes that the "bandying of words and phrases, arguing over definitions, and use of clichés, proverbs and truisms recalls Gustave Flaubert's *Bouvard et Pécuchet*", and adds between brackets "to which the title of the novel already suggests a debt".[28]

In her 1982 interview, Rachel Burrows recalls that during his lectures Beckett stressed the importance of Dostoevsky who created a literary "clair-obscur", with characters *"mal dégagés de l'ombre*" [partly still in shadow]. In Beckett's view, Proust and Gide were his natural successors because they too refused to distort the incomprehensibility of the real. And she adds: "He hated Balzac, of course. He hated what he called the snowball act, which means that you do something that has causes, causes, causes, causes so that it's all perfectly consistent." More specifically, what one finds in Rachel Burrows' notebook is "the snowball act", according to Beckett, described in the following manner: "*enchaînement mécanique, fatal, de circonstances* [fatal, mechanical chain of circumstances]. Arbitrary direction of material by artist. [. . .] No *imprévu* [unexpected]. No incredulity. No impulsion." (40) During his lectures, having stated what a novel should be, Beckett increasingly attacks Balzac, accusing him of not questioning either his thinking or the quality of his characterisation.

Another of Beckett's metaphors linked to the snowball image is that of the pool table on which the balls are perfectly arranged and sent in one direction or another according to a very precise strategy. For Beckett, on the contrary, as Ms Burrows says in her interview, art was the progressive discovery of the real: "The artist himself was changing all the time and his material was constantly in a state of flux, hence you had to do something to organize this mess, but not to make puppets and set them in motion, and not to fantasize in the way the Romantics did. He's concerned with digging into the real as he sees it at that moment, and even that was relative, because the artist is changing, the material is changing, and the moment is changing. So you see, you have absolutely nothing but his real aesthetics."

Rachel Burrows adds some interesting comments on this part of the course. She notes that it is clear what did and did not interest Becket from his earliest years. She recalls, for example, that "He loved the 'clair-obscure,' the light that comes in at one moment to leave the rest in shadow", and that he quoted Gide as saying "Balzac paints like David, Dostoevsky like Rembrandt." She asserts that "he saw Gide and Proust as the successors to Dostoevsky because they dared to preserve the complexity of the real, the inexplicable, unforeseeable quality of the human being", and that "he rejected the naturalistic novels of writers like Balzac, which only depict the surface which he said had been peeled off by Proust." And indeed, the student's notes refer to "Balzac's greatness": "power of transcribing surface, cataloguing, detail apprehended, but [concentrating one's] whole interest on surface, [which] makes one impatient [because it is] not interesting". (105)

Beckett had emphasized earlier why he did not consider Balzac to be a modern author: "[The] duality of Balzac [is] not *organic*. [It comprises] 2 separate things which don't interfere 1) Balzac: realistic notater 2) Balzac the romantic psychologist. [These] 2 aspects never affect each other. Modern novelist interested in neither but in organic state" – which of course does not rule out incoherence as a subject, quite the opposite. Flaubert, on the other hand, displays coherence in his duality, "[with] *L'Education sentimentale* [he is a] realistic notater [but also] *onomatomaniac*; [with] *Salammbô* and *La Tentation*, [he] suggests that [the] verbal fever is connected with [the] precision of [the] notater". And Beckett recapitulates: "[The] Inner precision [of a text is] contradictory. [The] Confusion irreducible. Final analysis, [the novel is] incoherent". (95)

Stendhal's appeal to Beckett appears to lie in his *deliberately* incoherent duality. According to him, Stendhal was both "an encyclopedist and mysticist with a particular conception of *bonheur*". These two aspects appeared "not side by side but [resulted in the] retrospective abolition of logical structure" of the narrative.[29] Beckett offers, by way of an example, Julien Sorel's "moment of ecstasy" (which he subsequently called "grace") in *Le Rouge et le noir [The Red and the Black]*, a moment which "abolishes patient structure" through the *"encyclopedantic machinery"* used by Stendhal, according to Beckett, who asserts that he is "not really interested in [the] illumination of it". And indeed, why would he be? "[The] *Bonheur* of grace [is] not [the result of] a logical endeavour", replies Beckett, it depends on the "intimate participation of the real and the ideal [which forms the] integral expression in Proust. Gide demands [that the] novel [should mix the] real and [the] ideal. What is and what should be. Proust says [that the] real material, whether approached empirically or imaginatively remains hermetic: when applied imaginatively, it is absent and lacks actual reality; when [it is] applied empirically (direct perception) [the] surface [is] also hermetic: a screen of self-consciousness [is] established by [the] subject between himself and the object (zone of evaporation between incandescent body and damp body, says Proust. No real tangency between subject and object). *[The] whole problem [lies here]: how to apprehend the real?* In a sense of [the notion of] grace which depends on [the] reduplication of [a] past sensation in the present, the ideal [is] real, not merely [a] function of present or past, but extra temporal. [The] participation between [the] real and [the] ideal [is the] entire Proustian solution. No such solution in Stendhal – incoherent entity of two components: one abolishes the other. They coexist in [a] state of incoherence. Another implication linking Stendhal with modern novelists [is the] implication that [the] psychological real can't be stated, [that it is] imperceptible from every point of view. [The] conclusion is negative." (97–99)

Beckett takes as an example two Stendhalian heroes, Fabrice del Dongo and Julien Sorel. Fabrice "first thinks he can be stated, then finds his reality can be satisfied by no value. [The] reality of

[the] material remains undetermined." Julien feels that "social value only satisfies [him] partly, [that he also cares for the] mystical value. When [he becomes] aware of being irreducibly complex [he decides that] only [the] multiplicity of values can satisfy his equation." (101) Beckett concludes: "[Stendhal has] a more intimate contact with modern thought" [than his contemporaries]. That made him more akin to the 20th-century writers "interested in [the] smallest known psychological components, [where] constituents are indeterminate" – unlike Balzac who is "only concerned with [the] majority of constituents, not with [the] minority that can't be valued or remain incoherent". (101)

In his introductory lecture on Gide, Beckett announces: "Influences: Flaubert, Stendhal". (3) This remark confirms that Beckett ranks Gide among the great contemporary authors. He sees in them what he considers to be an essential quality: the recognition of complexity (both of the human being/character and of writing), in contrast to the Romantics and the Naturalists who, in his view, are without this complexity, which can find different forms of expression. According to Beckett, Stendhal is more "concerned with [the] reaction of [the] character [than with the] circumstance", (3) whereas Flaubert is more concerned with the "circumstance reducing [the] character to banality". (5) Furthermore, in Flaubert he sees a "personal system of reference", rich and open to several possibilities. On the other hand, he criticises the Naturalists' "forced unification (Zola, etc.)" and the presence of a system of reference based on a single idea, a single attitude, from which complexity is excluded. Outlining Gide's literary background, Beckett describes the Romantics and the Naturalists as artificial, and the "prenaturalists" as authentically complex. After this brief introduction, he goes on to talk about the writers he himself admires – including Flaubert,

Stendhal, Rimbaud and Proust – arguing that the "postnatural-ists" (namely Paul Bourget, Anatole France, Pierre Loti, Maurice Barrès and André Gide) are similar to the prenaturalists because of their reaction to the Naturalists. (7) This group, he claims, had no system of reference in the strict sense but sought a balance between intelligence and intuition. Beckett lists three attributes that are the benchmark for innovativeness in modern writing: *"originalité, génialité, imprévisibilité"* [originality, genius, unpre-dictablilty]. He adds that the Symbolists and Dadaists adopted them and that they are thus the "last [to be] interested in this idea of inadequacy of the word to translate impressions registered by instinct". He suggests that Gide represents the "new incoher-ence" provoked by "[the] impatience with [the] patient[ly] fabricated order of [the] Romantics and [the] Naturalists". (9) At the end of his lecture, Beckett insists on the fact that the Proustian solution, which consists of grasping the real by making it collude with the ideal, is not that of Gide, quite the opposite. "No sacred communion between [the] real and [the] ideal" in the latter, according to Beckett. Where Gide is concerned, there is appar-ently: "only [one] conclusion, that his material can't be stated or valued or related to any valuable cause: [the] incoherence of it only can be stated". (103)

GIDE

Rudmose-Brown had taught Gide to the young Beckett and, on the latter's return from France, had given him several of his student groups. That said, it is not certain whether Beckett followed the same syllabus as his former professor. We have the distinct impression that Beckett had his own teaching approach. The content of his lectures reveals some of his preferences and reflections on the subject of literature.

Naturally the course began with the list of Gide's works. Here are a few extracts:

"*Si le grain ne meurt [If It Die]* describes Protestant background.

Characteristic strain: almost Jansenistic. One permanent element: search for God – encouraged by Dostoevsky.

First book. *Les Cahiers d'André Walter [The Notebooks of André Walter]*. Obsession for Evangelists, specially in Germany, First piece of dogmatism = doctrine of renunciation. Like a Christian Laforgue.

Les Nourritures terrestres [Fruits of the Earth]. Introduction to critic's work. Doctrine of '*vivre dangeureusement*' [living dangerously]:[30] rejection of moral and social control, *'passion et ferveur'* (dialogue with acolyte), stands alone. Rhapsodical style, generally sober."

In discussing *Le Voyage d'Urien [Urien's Voyage]*, Beckett shows that Gide had acquired his own individual style, bidding "farewell to symbolism". (10) Then he presents *La Porte étroite [Strait is the Gate]* "as an enlargement of *Les Nourritures terrestres*" once again emphasising "[the] value of risk, [the doctrine of] *vivre dangeureusement*". Alissa's character is shown in its duality, in a "mystical position", between the denial of temptation and a negative position. (13)

He moves on to *La Symphonie pastorale*, talks of three agents in conflict and describes the Protestant R.C. as passionate but not very perceptive, suggesting "[the] inability of happiness for an ignorant person": the reverend cannot confer happiness on a woman who has not sinned. (13) Here, Beckett mentions Nietzsche's influence on Gide. Then he tackles *Le Prométhée mal enchaîné [Prometheus Ill-bound]* speaking of "potential flight, dignity of individual eagle = symbol".

After this introduction, Beckett devotes a great deal of time to Dostoevsky's influence on Gide, in particular on *Les Caves du Vatican [The Vatican Cellars/Lafcadio's Adventure]*, *Les Faux-Monnayeurs [The Counterfeiters]*, *L'Immoraliste [The Immoralist]* and *Si le grain ne meurt*. According to Beckett, the effects of Gide's Protestant upbringing being deep-rooted, he was encouraged by what he found in Dostoevsky, in other words, the principle of renunciation – and Rachel Burrows noted: "Position of authentic individual to good neighbour" as opposed to the "anarchic nature of Catholicism".

Beckett analyses *Les Caves du Vatican*, whose hero, Lafcadio, decides to throw a man off a train. He stresses that Gide is interested in the "*crime immotivé*" [motiveless crime], in the "*intelligence passionnelle*" [emotive intelligence] – derived from Bergsonian "*imprévisibilité*" [unpredictability]. "Gide, according to Beckett, admired the mental conflict in Dostoevsky [and his] acceptance of [the] coexistence of apparently mutually exclusive states in the same organ." He also agrees with Dostoevsky's idea that "thought goes further than science" and that crime is "an act that cannot be reduced to motive." He insists on the other hand that the true source of the act is to be found not in the mind but in the nerves – for him, like a "modern Proust", Gide moves from the mind to the heart and nerves. (14)

Beckett was interested in Bergson's theory that "language can't express confusion". (16) In his view, apart from the Surrealists, only Gide insists "on [the] reconciliation between [the] authentic incoherence of post-Bergsonian thought and [the] coherence of Racinian statement," and infers from it that: "one doesn't reveal oneself in quality of one's thought but of one's expression" (17) – which leads Beckett to conclude that "style argues the man".

Beckett concludes: in Gide, there is a "development from Nietzsche through Dostoevsky to Racine – from assertion of *moi* to renunciation of *moi* to independence of *moi*."(17)

Beckett dwells at length on Gide's essay on Dostoevsky (*Dostoïevski.* "Articles et causeries")[31] and Rachel Burrows' notes show that he scrupulously follows the order of the essay chapters. For Beckett, this essay says a lot more about Gide than it does about Dostoevsky (rather like his own *Proust* which sets out literary principles that are more Beckettian than Proustian). At the start of the course, he recommended that his students "read Gide on Dostoevsky for Gide himself". (8) In this essay, which in fact draws together several articles and lectures from between 1908 and 1921, Gide underlines the "powerful complexity" which explains the Russian master's apparent confusion, that same confusion which alienates "Westerners such as Barrès or Balzac who love simplification" (another swipe at Balzac, in passing . . . this time coming from Gide).[32] On the contrary, in Dostoevsky, no "*solution bienséante*" [seemly solution] – what Gide calls "*la simplification de vulgarité*" [trite simplification], while denying any need for "uniformity of valid information". (19) Beckett told his students that Gide admired the "*caractère irraisonné, irrésolu, irresponsable*" [irrational, irresolute and irresponsible nature] of Dostoevsky's characters.[33]

For Gide – and Beckett places great emphasis on this point – the "*complexité problématique*" [problematic complexity] with which Dostoevsky creates his characters is the antithesis of Balzac for whom the "*souci principal semble être toujours la parfaite conséquence du personnage*" [main concern seems always to be the character's perfect consistency][34] – hence his "interest in explanations" and his meticulous preparation of the "sequence of character action", so as to make the plot "plausible". (21) Gide, on the other hand, wrote (this, the young student did not grasp clearly, but Beckett makes a point of quoting him): "I know no writer richer in contradictions and inconsistencies than Dostoevsky: Nietzsche would describe them as *antagonisms*." And Beckett concludes (and this is underlined in Rachel Burrows' notebook): "*Absurdity of getting to know yourself from [an] artistic point of view*". (21) By that, Gide effectively means that an author who is trying to get to know himself runs the risk of writing "coldly, deliberately, in keeping with the self he has found". Beckett also underlines Gide's remark that "the true artist is never but half-conscious of himself when creating".[35] And Gide adds immediately afterwards – and this is not in the notes – "He does not know exactly who he is".

Beckett's underlining of Gide's remark and his well-known refusal to explain his own work might suggest a tacit approval on his part.

Beckett identifies a crucial attribute that Gide has in common with Dostoevsky: the presence of Christian thought, characterised by humility, in their work. Beckett contrasts this thinking with the "artificial Romantic fabricated model", (21) which denies human complexity by making it understandable through mastering it in a certain way. He finds this trait, which he considers to be a form of arrogance, for example, in Nietzsche who, according to Gide, was jealous of Christ, and even tried to position himself as His victorious rival, whose teaching he claimed to supplant. On the contrary, explains Beckett basing himself on Gide's essay, humility permits Dostoevsky to bow before Him whose superiority he acknowledges, and the most important consequence of this submission is to preserve the complexity of human nature. Gide, in Beckett's view, is uncompromising with regard to anything that eradicates this complexity and thus flattens emotions and thoughts by refusing to acknowledge the incoherent or the inexpressible – he cites Balzac as representing the logical and linear narrative. (43) Rachel Burrows' notes show that Beckett places great emphasis on this aspect of Gide's thought: "*abnégation qui permet dans l'âme de Dostoïevski les sentiments contraires*" [sacrifice which makes it possible for contradictory feelings to exist in Dostoevsky's soul][36]. Later he points out too that Gide is interested in "liminal consciousness", in what "cannot be translated consciously – *abîme* to be respected", and that he "imparts quality to inconclusiveness (how can you conclude when some elements of [a] problem are not available and can't be considered?)" (43)

Beckett draws his students' attention to that fact that in Gide there is an "interesting distinction between [the] Western need

37

and [the] Russian need". (24) Rachel Burrows' notes liken this distinction to the differences between the Catholic and Orthodox Churches in Christianity identified by Gide. But this passage is too brief to satisfy us and we must refer to the original. Denying that he is "sacrificing, indeed immolating Balzac to Dostoevsky", as he has been accused of doing, Gide explains his preference for the latter: "With Balzac (as invariably in Western society, in French especially, to which his novels hold a mirror), two factors are active which in Dostoevsky's work practically do not exist; first, the intellect, second, the will." For Gide, many Balzacian heroes achieve virtue through willpower and make a glorious career as a result of perseverance and intelligence. Conversely, in Dostoevsky's work, as in the Gospel, the Kingdom of Heaven belongs to the poor in spirit. For him, the antithesis of love is less hate than the steady activity of the mind".[37] Gide considers Dostoevsky's resolute characters as "terrible creatures" and "his most dangerous characters are the strongest intellectually". And he concludes: "Balzac's *Comédie humaine* sprang from the contact between the Gospels and the Latin mind: Dostoevsky's from the contact between the Gospels and Buddhism" – this comment is summarised, mistakenly, in Burrows' lecture notes as "Stendhal + Dost. [The former] union of Saint John and RC orthodoxy. [The latter] Quietism Saint John and Greek Church, almost Buddhism, no anger."[38] (24) This difference was to prove of capital importance here as it enabled Beckett to develop a stylistic trait that would recur throughout his work: the use of the contrast between shadow and light.

Beckett told his students that Dostoevsky was far removed from Stendhal for whom the novel was a *"miroir sur un chemin"* [mirror on a path]. (27) He picked up on one of Gide's ideas – and this only received a brief mention in Rachel Burrows' notes –, the notion that Dostoevsky's technique is that of painting, whereas in

Stendhal, it is that of panorama: "Dostoevsky composes a picture in which the most important consideration is the question of light. The light proceeds from but one source. In one of Stendhal's novels, the light is constant, steady, and well-diffused. But in Dostoevsky's books, as in a Rembrandt portrait, the shadows are the essential. Dostoevsky groups his characters and happenings, plays a brilliant light upon them, illuminating one aspect only. Each of his characters has a deep setting of shadow, reposes on its own shadow almost."[39] Beckett adds to this observation: "no explanations in Dostoevsky".

He then presents *La Porte étroite* as a good example of the contrast between shadow and light, through the "unexplained mysticism of Alissa", "paradox of Evangelistic renunciation: save life and lose it". And he states that: "If Balzac treated this, he'd establish [a] train of motives and explain it all". (27)

What follows in Rachel Burrows' notes again relates to Gide's essay on Dostoevsky, but in a rather muddled manner (in a lecture situation, it is common for students to lose the thread of the quotes). What Gide actually says is that, in Dostoevsky, there is always a moment when events interweave and take confused form like in a vortex; the elements of the story – moral, psychological and material – disappear and reappear in this whirlpool. With him there is never any attempt to straighten out or simplify; he is at home in complexity and even protects it.[40] Rachel Burrows adds Beckett's comment that Dostoevsky "refuses to distort reality [. . .] *No abstraction*: ideas [are the] function of [the] character – *human* and *inexplicable*." (29) Here, Beckett was probably thinking of Jacques Rivière's article, published in the *Nouvelle Revue Française* of 1st February 1922 and cited by Gide in his essay, where he contends that Dostoevsky respects and even protects the dark side of his characters, and is interested primarily in their *abîmes*, while the French novelists "faced with the complexity almost every human being offers", seek to order it: "At need, we force things a trifle; we suppress a few small divergences, and interpret certain obscure details in the sense most useful towards establishing a psychological unity. The ideal we strive towards is the complete closing up of every gulf." And Gide takes Balzac as an example, which must doubtless have pleased Beckett: "His one concern was to produce characters free of all inconsequences, wherein he was in perfect accord with French feeling; for what we French require most of all is logic."[41] Gide adds that, in Balzac, there is undoubtedly "much that he fails to explain" but not "much that could not be explained". On the other hand, Dostoevsky, "the dwelling place of conflicting feelings" seems "the more paradoxical in that his characters' feelings are forced to their extremist intensity and exaggerated to the point of absurdity."

Beckett returns to this notion, which for him is primordial, and tells his students: "You can either respect a cavern or go about it with an electric torch as Stendhal or Balzac". We note, for the second time, that Beckett did not have only good things to say about Stendhal.[42] And so, when it comes to lack of contrast, Stendhal is ranked alongside Tolstoy and also Balzac. Beckett grants that the modern French novel is aware of "artificial unification of character." Nevertheless, he observes that "[the] French dread [the] lack of form and shape", and points out the absence in their novels of children – characters that are potentially hard to pin down – unlike Dostoevsky who is "full of children". (29)

It is perhaps through Gide that Beckett discovered Dostoevsky. He was not on the Trinity College syllabus, and Beckett, who was an admirer of Gide at the time, is bound to have delved into the sources that influenced the novelist. It is also likely that he encountered him through Proust, since Dostoevsky's name comes up several times in Beckett's essay: for example, "Proust can be related to Dostoevsky, who states his characters without explaining them. It may be objected that Proust does little else but explain his characters. But his explanations are experimental and not demonstrative. He explains them in order that they may appear as they are – inexplicable."[43] Whether it is through Gide and/or Proust, or not, it is worth noting that when he recommends that his students read Dostoevsky, Beckett gives the title of the novel in French – *L'Eternel mari* [*The Eternal Husband*], for example. (28) Elsewhere, in a letter to MacGreevy, he speaks of a Dostoevsky novel that he is reading and again gives the title in French, *Les Possédés [The Possessed]*.[44] So we have the distinct impression that Beckett read, at least in part, the Russian novelist's works in French translation. Apparently he planned to write an essay on Dostoevsky in the 1930s, and Anthony Cronin, another biographer of Beckett, suggests that in 1931 Beckett offered it to Chatto and Windus, the London publishing house which had already published his *Proust* in the "Dolphin Books" series, but to no avail.

As we have seen, Gide agrees with Dostoevsky on the principle of "the action devoid of outer motive" and, citing the Russian novelist: "a life should not be wasted in pursuit of a goal". (23) The reasons behind the characters' actions are not identified, and they are definitely not social. "*Les idées ne sont jamais absolues, [elles sont] relatives aux personnages et aux mouvements précis de la vie de ces personnages*" [The ideas are never absolute, [they are] relative to the characters and the precise movements in the lives of these characters], notes Rachel Burrows. These are no more than "series of moments", which makes each of them inaccessible to the others. (25)

However, Beckett finds a coherence in Gide despite the precepts he sets out. No "*foisonnement confus*" [unruly abundance], as in Dostoevsky. This difference can perhaps be explained by

Gide's Protestantism, [he is a] "Protestant in all that French Protestantism implies", adds Beckett who draws on the portrayal of childhood at the beginning of Gide's memoirs, *Si le grain ne meurt*: "Grave, rather deviate, tutor not school, reads philosophers not Bible, very intelligent, almost frightened by abilities." (44) Beckett stated earlier that "Protestantism explains most of his [Gide's] characters". (37)

With *Les Faux-Monnayeurs*, which was one of the set books, Beckett enters into the quick of the matter. He asserts that for Gide it is an attempt to renew the traditional structure of the novel. In Beckett's view, Gide is "most self-conscious, self-critical of great artists – in common with Flaubert and Dostoevsky, yet exempt from [their] spontaneity and passionate heart." According to Beckett, Gide is: "Aware and tragically so of what he is *not* doing". However, he also points out that Gide called three of his works – *Paludes*, *Le Prométhée mal enchaîné* and *Les Caves du Vatican* – "soties", (31) which denotes the presence of satirical, even consciously farcical elements in Gide that must have appealed to Beckett. Self-criticism and criticising contemporary society are two aspects of Gide's work which Beckett identifies and sees operating at different levels, in particular in *Les Faux-Monnayeurs*. (52)

What was Gide trying to do? "Protestant iconoclast, [Gide] rejects [the] realistic novel and [the] analytical novel (killed by Proust). [He] seeks [a] new narrative form, [which might be] analytical without being demonstrative, interrogative not conclusive, epic without being descriptive", replies Beckett. And he explains to his students that the narrative structures of the French novel (of the time) follow those of 19th-century drama: giving the reader clues and "setting [. . .] characters in motion like machines", to a rhythm uninterrupted by any complexity whatsoever. Gide, on the other hand, he claims, introduces new

42

questions into each of his novels.

In *Paludes*, which has "[the] genius and [the] originality of *Les Faux-Monnayeurs*," (33) according to Beckett, "[the] action, instead of being treated methodically, is treated symphonically. [The] interest [resides] in [the] potential, in [the] milieu". Beckett applauds the portrayal of characters whose actions once carried out restrict those they could have undertaken. The novel, far from being an exposition, is a gradual discovery of the real. What Beckett stresses most emphatically, and which seems to interest him at the deepest level, is the idea that Gide denies the importance of the consciously useful gesture, and devotes himself instead to the gratuitous act (that of *Prometheus*, for example).

Les Faux-Monnayeurs was central to the course, and, according to Beckett "[the] greatest book since Proust". (53) He presents the novel's various elements to the students:

"Objective statement of characters.

Intervention of Edouard (author, partly Gide) . . . 'Journal d'Edouard' comments as [a] spectator.

Edouard's judgement [examined] in turn by various characters.

Edouard no longer spectator – involved in action by interest in young man.

No conclusive gesture or judgement in book [. . .]; no absolute value, different on each plane." (35)

Beckett then pinpoints the innovative traits in *Les Faux-Monnayeurs*. First of all, he goes back to the idea that it is an "analytical novel refusing to commit itself to conclusions". Then he examines the ambiguity of the title, not without having emphasised that it is a "novel writing a novel: 1) *Les Faux-Monnayeurs* [is] Edouard's idea as title for his novel, 2) may apply to a group of schoolboys, 3) to [the] falsification of art (represented by artist), 4) to [the] falsification of education (satire on *lycée*)".

Beckett informs his students that "Gide [is] preserving [the] integrity of incoherence", and quotes him: "*les tendances les plus opposées n'ont jamais réussi à faire de moi un tourmenté. Cet état de dialogue qui pour tant d'autres est à peu près intolérable devenait pour moi nécessaire* (antagonistic dialogue)" [the most contradictory tendencies have never made me anguished. This kind of dialogue, which for so many others is almost intolerable, became necessary for me][37].

"[In Gide the] struggle between [the] artist and [the] idea must be incorporated in [the] novel," states Beckett, and once again he contrasts him with Balzac: "Gide refuses to abdicate as critic even in [his] novel. [. . .] Turns to impulse. Action [is] only interesting as suggesting the multiple probable potentials. *Insistence on free will* (*Les Faux-Monnayeurs*: free will of creator and of creatures). For Balzac, characters can't change their minds or its [the novel's] artistic structure crashes". (41) "Petrification, immobilisation, etc. [were] words hated by Gide", adds Beckett. (42)

At the end of the lecture he sums up the key points his students should remember concerning Gide and *Les Faux-Monnayeurs*, in particular:

1) Protestant
2) Iconoclast
3) Influences of Nietzsche and Dostoevsky
4) Understanding Bergson (*symphonie* not *mélodie*; treatment of depth not of surface).

He also reminds them that Gide is "no more interested in Naturalists than Proust", their distinctive characteristic being to create a novel that mirrors nature but which is only superficial.

Gide prefers the "apparent injustice" of the classics. (45) Beckett uses *Les Faux-Monnayeurs* to illustrate the author's opinions, as conveyed through the character of Edouard: "Is it because the novel, of all literary *genres*, is the freest, the most *lawless*, [. . .] is it for that very reason, for fear of that very liberty (the artists who are always sighing after liberty are often the most bewildered when they get it), that the novel has always clung to reality with such timidity? [. . .] The only progress it looks to is to get still nearer to nature. The novel has never known that 'formidable erosion of contours', as Nietzsche calls it; that deliberate avoidance of life, which gave style to the works of the Greek dramatists, for instance, or to the tragedies of the French seventeenth century. Is there anything more perfectly and deeply human than these works? But that's just it – they are human only in their depths; they don't pride themselves on appearing so – or, at any rate, on appearing real. They remain works of art."[45] (47)

Confirming this preference of Gide's, Beckett continues to cite Edouard: "Sometimes it seems to me there is nothing in all literature I admire so much as, for instance, the discussion between Mithridate and his two sons in Racine; it's a scene in which the characters speak in a way we know perfectly well no father and no sons could ever have spoken in, and yet (I ought to say for that very reason) it's a scene in which all fathers and all sons can see themselves. By localizing and specifying one restricts. It is true that there is no psychological truth unless it be particular; but on the other hand there is no art unless it be general."[46] And Beckett adds, to drive the point home: "Balzac expresses [the] general at the expense of [the] particular". (48)

On the question of the novel's subject, still using Edouard as a mouthpiece, Beckett demonstrates how Gide attacks the Naturalist school: "It [the novel] hasn't got one [subject][. . .] 'a slice of life', the naturalist school said. The great defect of that school is that it always cuts its slice in the same direction; in time, lengthwise. Why not in breadth? Or in depth? As for me I should like not to cut at all. Please understand; I should like to put everything into my novel."[47] (50)

According to Beckett, Gide is "afraid of the liberty which he is forced to give his characters and wishes to escape from *le réel*, but holds himself back." His writing depicts "that very struggle between what reality offers him and what he himself desires to make of it."[48] Beckett cites *Les Faux-Monnayeurs* again: "Well, I should like a novel which should be at the same time as true and as far from reality, as particular and at the same time as general, as human and as fictious as *Athalie*, or *Tartuffe* or *Cinna*."[49] (51) However, at the end of his course on Racine, Beckett returns briefly to Gide to say that his antagonisms are not as "subtle or singular" as those of the master and that, in Gide, unlike Racine, "[the] mind [is] in flux, [never] resolved." (79)

Before starting to teach at Trinity, Beckett had made copious notes on Gide and was thinking of writing an essay on him to be published by Chatto and Windus, who had published his *Proust*. But they were not interested in this project. In 1932, Beckett tried his luck once again, this time with Ellis Roberts, chief editor of the *New Statesman*. Roberts agreed to publish an article of around 1800 words on Gide's entire oeuvre, but nothing longer. Unable to work in his family home, Beckett abandoned the project at the draft stage, even though he had come up with a promising subtitle, "Paralysed in ubiquity".[50] He could still have found a publisher in 1937, in Houghton Mifflin, an American publishing house which had shown little enthusiasm for his novel *Murphy* and had already turned down *Proust* a few years earlier, finding it too short to be published on its own. This time, Houghton Mifflin offered to take it and publish it along with other essays to make a more substantial book. These would have included, in addition to Proust and Gide, Beckett's writings on Céline and Malraux, authors whom he had also read and admired.[51] Too depressed by the poor reception *Murphy* received at the time, Beckett could not imagine himself working on another book, and declined the offer. This chapter therefore brings together some of the notes made by Beckett in preparation for the essay on Gide, and gives us an idea of what he might have done with them.

To follow the logical development in Beckett's thinking, it is worth noting that in his lecture on Gide, he mentions the importance of Racine in Gide's most recent work at the time, *L'Ecole des femmes [The School for Wives]* (1929). In it he sees a "painful restraint of language and method" adopted by the author, "getting back to Racine" and returning "towards classicism". Beckett comments that Gide had "let himself go in *Les Nourritures terrestres* ([with] some unfortunate results)", but that "for the rest", he considered "restraint a sacrifice of [the] thinker". (15) From the stylistic viewpoint, Beckett states that Gide is always "faithful to classical litotes" (39) and cites him again: *"Je bannis de mon style toute emphase; Il n'y a pas de pire ennemi de la pensée que le démon d'analogie"* [I banish all pomposity from my style; the devil of analogy is the worst enemy of thought]. Furthermore, he contends that Gide *"ne perdit jamais de vue l'idéal classique"* [never lost sight of the classical ideal] and that he identified, apparently, with the compromise between individual thinking and social position. And Rachel Burrows underlined: "[The] Classical artist is most intensely individual". (15)

Beckett further compares Gide and Racine on two other points: their treatment of time (he claims there is none in Racine) and the psychological conclusion (he argues that there is none in Gide, no more than there is "absolute clarity"). Beckett, according to the notes, explains to his class that the complexity of Racine's characters has a material function, that of creating the time and place of the action, and underlines the "potential validity of any given gesture". (52)

Rachel Burrows thinks that Beckett was interested above all in Proust, Gide and Dostoevsky, the great master of complexity. She maintains that, while the syllabus was drawn up by the French faculty, the content of the course, on the other hand, was chosen by Beckett: "but he would obviously stress the things that appealed to him. I think that Dostoevsky was not required but certainly Gide and Proust were, so probably, in dealing with Gide and Proust and the modern novel, he would have taken what he thought were the predecessors like Dostoevsky, you see. And then he would link that up with Racine, which was also set." Now we shall see that Beckett's interest in Racine was greater than Rachel Burrows suspected.

DRAMA

TRADITION VERSUS
EXPERIMENTATION

In drama, as in the novel, Beckett admired the writers who portrayed human complexity and approached their art in an innovative manner: Synge, Pirandello, Strindberg and Chekhov, for example. He was very quickly drawn to European experimental theatre and later counted Harold Pinter among his friends. As a student at Trinity College, he had discovered French classical drama – Molière, Corneille and Racine – as well as Marivaux. Racine's very modernity remained a source of inspiration for Beckett and in his teaching, in 1931, he demonstrated this modernity by taking counter-examples: Corneille, of course, Racine's great rival, but also, repeatedly, Balzac.

It was Rudmose-Brown who fired Beckett's appreciation of Racine. He read all his plays which made a lasting impression on him. Knowlson suggests that Rudmose-Brown "strongly influenced Beckett's own tastes in literature and undoubtedly affected his attitudes to life. It was he who inspired Beckett with his deep love for Racine's plays but equally passed on to him his antipathy to Corneille's".[52] In her interview, Rachel Burrows also mentions that "Professor Rudmose-Brown had such admiration for his junior lecturer that he gave him his lectures on Racine, which he usually took himself. Beckett shared his liking for Racine and his dislike for the heroics of Corneille". She remembers his insistence on "the subconscious in Racine" and "his pinpointing the solitary nature of every human being. In his essay on Proust, [. . .] he said 'We are alone. We cannot know and we cannot be known', a theory which could be applied to his own work."[53]

What interested Beckett above all in Racine's plays is that little happens. In his preface to *Bérénice*, to defend himself from those who accused him of lack of action in his theatre, Racine himself stated that he sought simplicity: "Only what is probable can move us in a tragedy. And what is there probable about a multitude of things happening in one day which could hardly happen in several weeks? There are some who think that this simplicity is a sign of lack of invention. They do not reflect that on the contrary *all invention consists in making something out of nothing.*"[54] A phrase of Beckett's from *Malone Dies* immediately comes to mind: "*Nothing is more real than nothing*". Vivian Mercier, commenting on the two acts of *Waiting for Godot,* pointed out that it was "a play in which nothing happens, *twice*".[55] Knowlson suggests that *Ill Seen Ill Said* also contains allusions to Racine, and Mercier that Beckett's neoclassicism has been recognised by only a handful of French and English critics. It is true that Beckett's plays, in common with Racine's tragedies, have unity of time, place and action, and that the characters in both of their work often function in pairs.[56]

Beckett would certainly have been aware of Gide's comparison of Corneille to Dostoevsky. According to Gide, the contradictory feelings that inhabit the novelists' characters are not to be found in the dramatist's work: "The French hero, as

Corneille depicts him, throws before himself the image of an ideal: there is not a little of himself in it, himself as he desires and strives to be, not as Nature made him, or as he would be if he yielded to his instincts."[57] – which Gide associates with Bovarysm. Among the French playwrights able to portray a character's duality and contradictions, Gide too cites Racine, which perhaps reinforced Beckett's own view.

According to Rachel Burrows, the reason Beckett loathed Corneille and why he produced *Le Kid*, a skit on the dramatist, "was that he felt that Corneille was utterly artificial. He was distorting the real by his heroics, showing people as they were meant to be. Racine, on the other hand, painted men as they were. Within the framework of classicism, he was extraordinarily modern, and Sam loved finding little bits of what he called 'liminal consciousness,' rather than the subconscious, within Racine." Rachel Burrows recalls that, in Beckett's view, the pure subconscious cannot be used in literature – that "would destroy the integrity of the real, whereas 'liminal consciousness,' the half of consciousness, that was the thing he really wanted."[58]

Le Kid (1931) is the first play Beckett wrote in French. He collaborated with Georges Pelorson, French *lecteur* at Trinity that year and a friend of Beckett's from his time at rue d'Ulm. It was a parody of Corneille's *Le Cid* performed at the Peacock Theatre, Dublin, as part of Trinity College Modern Languages Society's annual review. It was Beckett who thought up the title; he had developed an early interest in the cinema, and was a great Chaplin fan. Although the programme describes the play as a "Cornelian nightmare", the tone is burlesque. The set features a giant clock painted on a backdrop, with moving hands which an actor turns. Beckett plays the part of Don Diègue, an old man with a white beard holding an alarm clock. In the first act, he has a long monologue which he recites, while at the back of the stage the hands on the clock face turn, slowly at first, then faster and faster, keeping pace with the monologue. In the middle of the speech "*Ô rage ! ô désespoir ! ô vieillesse ennemie !*" [Oh rage! Oh despair! Oh age, my enemy!], the alarm goes off. He stops it and speeds up his delivery, but the alarm goes off again. The hands turn faster and faster. Beckett shouts at top speed. His speech has degenerated into an absurd series of incoherent phrases and syllables. The particular rhythm and speed of his rant is such that, years later, people who had seen *Le Kid* talked about the strange feeling they experienced the first time they heard Lucky's tirade in *Waiting for Godot*. And the alarm clock resurfaced in *Endgame*.

The treatment of time is a central preoccupation in *Le Kid*. It is easy to recognise here one of the major questions of classical drama, that of the unity of time: how to connect the two different times inherent in any theatrical performance, the objective duration of the play and the supposed duration of the action? In the interests of verisimilitude, it was agreed that the duration of the action should not exceed twenty-four hours. The duration thus compressed (the hands spinning faster and faster) created the necessary tension for the tragic ending (*Le Kid* concludes with a barman telling his customers that he is closing). Each act corresponded to the actual duration of the action, while intervening developments were supposed to take place during the intervals. Pelorson and Beckett thus mixed the constraints of classical drama with surrealist elements of their own time (costumes, props, movements, music, etc.). While this exercise could be hailed as avant-gardism (which Beckett had discovered during his stay in Paris), it should however be remembered that Pelorson himself described it as an "intellectual canular".[59]

It is possible that, for Beckett, *Le Kid* was a criticism of a certain traditional mindset, of the lack of experimentation in Corneille in particular. He returned to the subject with his first play, *Eleutheria*.[60] In the lecture on Gide, Beckett already mentioned Corneille, likening him to Balzac: "Corneille/Balzac abdicate as critics vs [unlike] Racine". (48)

RACINE

Mercier confirms that Beckett's favourite dramatist was Racine: "Beckett has studied the work of Racine more closely than that of any other dramatist, Shakespeare included".[61] In her interview, Rachel Burrows states that, of all Beckett's lectures, the ones on Racine remain etched in her memory: "you see, he was fascinated by this 'modernity' he found in Racine. One quotation in particular I remember about Andromaque: 'A loves B, and B loves C, and C loves D. The great pagan tiger of sexuality chasing its tail in outer darkness,' which is pure Sam Beckett. I think it's absolutely marvellous."

The lecture she remembers with such pleasure is at the beginning of her notes on Racine, the first play on the syllabus to be studied in detail being *Andromaque*. Beckett begins by underlining once again the importance of the characters' complexity, contrasting for the first time Racine with Corneille. Racine's characters are presented as solitary beings, with individual needs; in other words, they do not share these needs with anyone else. Beckett states: "No heroic love. [It is the] first time [that] sexuality [is] treated realistically." Beckett sees a gap "between this psychological realism and Corneille – no heroics here, confession and self-awareness [instead]". For Beckett, *Andromaque* is the "most terrible play of Racine", it has "none of [the] gaiety of *Phèdre* and *Athalie* (Leonine gaiety of Theseus)", the "tragic conflict [is to be] associated without being unified." "Darkness, cruelty, hate of sexuality [are] stated for [the] first time on [the] French stage. [The] Great pagan tiger of sexuality [is] chasing its tail in outer darkness." In the margin, Rachel Burrows draws a circle (had Beckett himself drawn one on the blackboard?) with the simple commentary "Situation. Circle". His explanation: "Oreste arrives and finds Hermione engaged to Pyrrhus; Pyrrhus is interested in Andromaque; Andromaque interested in Hector; Hector [is] dead. Circle: Oreste annexing Hermione, Hermione Pyrrhus, Pyrrhus Andromaque, Andromaque Hector or Astyanax". (57) Then, a brief presentation of the characters drawn from Greek mythology.

The notes on Racine are taken differently from those on Gide: even-numbered pages give numerous citations illustrating the textual analysis. For example, opposite page 57 which considers the antagonisms in the play, namely that between hatred and love, page 56 contains: "Act I Scene 4. [Pyrrhus to Andromaque who rejects him] '. . . *il faut désormais que mon cœur,/ S'il n'aime avec transport, haïsse avec fureur.*'" [Henceforth my heart, since it no more/Can love intensely, must intensely hate].[62] And to show that hatred triumphs over love: "Act I Scene 1. [Oreste speaking to Pylade about Hermione and his changed feelings] '*Je pris tous mes transports pour des transports de haine./ Détestant ses rigueurs, rabaissant ses attraits,/ Je défiais ses yeux de me troubler jamais./ Voilà comment je crus étouffer ma tendresse/ [. . .]. Puisque après tant d'efforts ma résistance est vaine, / Je me livre en aveugle au destin qui m'entraîne./ J'aime : je viens chercher Hermione en ces lieux,/ La fléchir, l'enlever ou mourir à ses yeux'.*"

[I fancied all my ferment sprang from hate;/Cursing her pride and whittling down her beauty,/I challenged her to trouble me again./And thus I thought to smother all my love./[. . .] Since all my strivings to resist are vain,/My destiny now sweeps me blindly on./ I love: and come to seek Hermione,/To win her, snatch her, or else die before her.]

Beckett's view is that Racine's characters have no sense of duty, but instead pursue their desires: "Andromaque would not have been faithful to Hector if she had been attracted by Pyrrhus"; "Hermione, if she can't annex Pyrrhus will make him suffer", and he adds "Madness of desire". Beckett considers this lack of moral obligation as another sign of modernity. He analyses the relationships between the characters as follows: Pyrrhus, envious of Andromaque's love for the son she had with Hector, tries to arouse her jealousy by going back to Hermione; Oreste takes this change of heart for cruelty towards him; blinded by her fury, Hermione wants Pyrrhus dead, but she also wants him to know who is killing him, in other words herself, by the hand of Oreste. (59) Hermione takes advantage of Oreste's love to murderous ends. The exploitation of some characters by others is incidentally the only political aspect of the play. According to Beckett, politics in Racine (unlike Corneille) are "hardly mentioned". Racine distanced himself from social issues to concentrate on the mind. (75)

In *Andromaque* Beckett identifies a constant relationship between cause and effect, which he sees as the expression of consciousness rather than of a critical stance: "[The] mind can't find [a] solution. When it's put up to Andromaque to find [a] solution from antagonisms [she wants to die to avoid marrying Pyrrhus, but she is afraid that to do so will seal her son's fate], her mind does not find [a] solution [. . .]. At what point in [the] self-consciousness does [the] play come to an end? When [the] mind faces facts, when [the] mind has an integral awareness of [the] facts [. . .], when there's [a] unification of awareness [. . .]. The conversations between [the characters and their] confidents [only offer a] fragmentary awareness. [Their] function [is] to express [the] division in [the] mind of [the] antagonists." (63) In the margin, she has written: "[when the] mind is unified [the] play ends. No physical action."

Beckett states that Racine can treat consciousness artistically because he "accepted things and could be an artist: they bestowed peace on him". In his work, "[there is] Nothing but [the] psychology of love – no other issues. [He] understood this and knew he did. Living amongst things which don't require him to doubt [. . .], not [living] amongst mysteries. So he can be self-conscious without being sceptical – can use art to express his equilibrium." (65)

Earlier, in his course on Gide, Beckett had underlined the *polylogue* technique, indicating a discussion between more than two people. (53) The conversation about the novel in *Les Faux-Monnayeurs*, which Beckett analysed and which gave Gide a mouthpiece for his precepts on the art of writing, involved four characters: Edouard, Sophroniska, Bernard and Laura. This technique is based on a simple principle, similar to that of the didactic dialogue, where one of the characters, in replying to the questions of the others, allows the author to elaborate on a particular topic. *Les Faux-Monnayeurs* uses the devices of the diary and of the *polylogue*, which complement each other in confessional literature.

Beckett draws a parallel between Gide and Racine. The dramatist uses the dialogue between the protagonists and their confidants to reveal the main characters' divided selves. The confidants' questions, exclamations and objections echo the misgivings in the minds of the protagonists, forcing them to confront those misgivings. Pyrrhus, for example, exposes his dilemma, between "lust for vengeance and lust for passion", in his dialogues with Phœnix and Andromaque. When fragmentation gives way to the meeting of minds, we have an integral view of the situation and it is the dénouement: "Then [it is the] catastrophe [and the] play ends". (65)

Hermione, realising that she must kill Pyrrhus herself and die, accepts her own fate, her mind clear. Since she cannot live with him, she prefers that they die together. Andromaque did not need to reappear; all that she desired had been expressed with sufficient clarity in her previous dialogues with her confidante for the audience to know how she would react to Pyrrhus's death.

Towards the end of the play, the confusion having been dispelled, there is no longer any need for dialogue. Oreste, in the penultimate scene, speaks of all his suffering, in a lucid soliloquy. On the other hand, such acute insight in the face of Hermione's ultimate rejection (he killed Pyrrhus to win her love) damages his reason: "[The] inner integrity that precedes [a] collapse [is the] tragedy of [the] clairvoyants," says Beckett. (67) The play ends with Oreste losing his mind.

For Beckett, "*[When] art [is] didactic to this extent [it] lifts [one's] own personal impression to [the] level of absolute values.* Nowadays [one's] own personal impressions can't be lifted to [the level of] absolute values: [the] only way to approach art is as an instrument that will unearth absolute values which no longer pre-exist. [The] Artistic statement has to uncover them: [it is] no longer a statement but a discovery." (67)

The essential aspect of Racine's modernity remains, in Beckett's view, "[the] explicit statement of [the] complex – [see the dialogues between] Pyrrhus and Phœnix and [between] Oreste and his friend [Pylade] (repetition of [the] hate motive towards Andromaque and Hermione)" (69) – a motive constantly accompanied by its opposite. And Beckett cites Oreste (Act I: Scene 1): "*Je sentis que ma haine allait finir son cours,/ Ou plutôt je sentis que je l'aimais toujours*" [I felt my hatred dwindle with my wrong,/Or rather I felt I loved her all along], and Hermione (Act IV: Scene 3): "*Que je le hais, enfin Seigneur [. . .]./ S'il ne meurt aujourd'hui, je puis l'aimer demain*" [That I detest him: [. . .] If he's not dead today, I may tomorrow/Love him once more]. (68)

The Racinian stage set, according to Beckett, "provides [the] reader with a graded depth of background. *Andromaque*: 1) Troy – smoke, blood, Hector, Priam. 2) Almost mythological palace and sea: "*Je sais de ce palais tous les détours obscurs,/ Vous voyez que la mer en vient battre les murs*" [I know the dim recesses of this palace/You see the waves caress its very walls]. All to create [an] atmosphere, not explicating background of Balzac." On the other hand, as Rachel Burrows notes, the Racinian character is a "victim of fatality, can't be explained. Troy, etc. give substance and harmonies to living characters worth more than their face value. [The] depth of character [is] as overtone is to note." Then Beckett compares Racine and Balzac: "[with] Racine [the] occasional absence of [the] characters gives [a] glimpse of [the] background. [With] Balzac [the] protagonist [is] devoured, annexed by [the] background." (69)

Rachel Burrows' notes reveal that in Beckett's opinion "[the] only interesting use of background is [the] perspective, [the] country into which one is pleased to think the figure may recede but from which the present emerged." (70) He briefly alludes to Leonardo da Vinci and the Florence school, adding: "Racine throws his light on the front of the stage where the protagonist is. Balzac behind." (73)

Lastly, Beckett gives a detailed analysis of the characters and begins by reiterating that their essence lies in antagonism:

"a) Andromaque. 1) (to confidant, i.e. herself, dramatic convenience to express inner discussion). Troy [is her] in-mind picture, [which corresponds to the] first aspect of Pyrrhus, i.e. [her] imaginary fidelity to Hector and [her] real love for Astyanax. 2) [The] necessity for keeping Astyanax alive will continue till their two poles merge into one, [till the] antagonisms become unity". For Beckett, "Andromaque [is] the least interesting character" of the play – this apparently harsh judgment can perhaps be explained by the fact that Andromaque is also the least complex character, her integrity being explicit at the beginning.

"b) Hermione. 1) [Her] vanity [is] exasperated by [her] loathing for Andromaque (III:4, Andromaque pleads [for her son] to Hermione) and [by the] arrival of Oreste (II:1, can't tolerate exposure before him). 2) [Her] tendency towards Pyrrhus [is] real[ly] mad.

c) Pyrrhus. Subtle, polarised mind. 1) Lust for Andromaque. 2) Hate for Andromaque (II:5).

d) Oreste. 1) Hopes for Hermione 2) Despairs of Hermione. Fatality and injustice." (73)

Beckett considers Act II of *Andromaque* is the "finest act in classical theatre". It reveals what precipitates the characters "to [the] final state of mind: [the] dynamic of [the] mind, [the] stasis of the mind, then [the] catastrophe". The characters, all trying to obtain something from each other, their purposes being forever irreconcilable, oscillate between desire and loathing, calm and anger. For Beckett, Act II demonstrates both Racine's perfect mastery of the classical conventions and his modernity. At the beginning of Act II for example, he comments on Hermione's guilt vis-à-vis Oreste, as follows: "'*C'est cet amour payé de trop d'ingratitude*' [It is this very love, so ill-requited]: first piece of sentimental psychology, searchlight on [the] kind of mind absent formerly from French Literature". (75)

The next play on the syllabus is *Phèdre*. Beckett begins with a presentation of Jansenism, "limiting man's free will". Then, he comments on Racine's preface and contends that his words on the "virtues, vices and the didactic nature of theatre [are nothing but] eyewash". "Does he expect [his] audience to take this seriously?" he asks again referring to Racine's phrase *"En effet, Phèdre n'est ni tout à fait coupable, ni tout à fait innocente [. . .] son crime est plutôt une punition des Dieux qu'un mouvement de sa volonté"* [In fact, Phaedra is neither altogether guilty nor altogether innocent [. . .] her crime is rather a punishment of the gods than of her own volition].[63] And in the margin, Rachel Burrows writes: "Last paragraph [on] virtue. [Racine is] pulling our leg". (78)

Why does Beckett question Racine's good faith and what does he see in *Phèdre*? He tells his students that "Racine's private life [is] mysterious 1675–1677 [when *Phèdre* appears for the first time]", that "something happened": in his view, *Phèdre* was the first of Racine's plays to contain "[a] sense of sin". These feelings are not evident in *Andromaque*. "In *Phèdre*, there appears to be one [a moral question] and Phèdre is aware of it": Beckett wonders if it is Racine's reconciliation with Jansenism that explains this new element. He also mentions Racine's twelve-year silence between *Phèdre* and his next play, *Esther*. (79)

After these reflections, he returns to Phèdre's culpability, maintaining that it is not real (nothing actually took place between her and her stepson, Hippolyte) but that Phèdre perceives it as such. For Beckett, the play is another study of the human mind and passion, which is more repressed than ever here in Racine. (79) "[It is a] purely cerebral [approach]," says Beckett, Racine is "interested in repressed passion [. . .] when forced underground to [the] darkness of the mind. Mutual affections, purely polite, don't interest him". (81) And he concludes that Racine is more interested in Bajazet than in Bérénice.

This passion represents for Beckett "[a] fever that can't be stated or realised". He goes back to the example of "Oreste obsessed by Hermione who is not even aware of him, except as possible lever [while] Pyrrhus [is] not aware of Hermione". Beckett then emphasises the idea that *"Final statement of Racinian thesis: that there is no impact*; they [the characters] are all *hermétiques*, not aware of each other, but of one thing: each trying to get into the other's state of mind. Hermione's plan of murder [against Pyrrhus] carries [the] thesis: [it is] no good murdering him if she can't get into his mind. Pyrrhus [. . .]: obsessed by Andromaque and she is only obsessed by a memory."[64] (81) And Beckett cites the clearest example of this lack of communication between the characters, the scene in which Hermione protests after Pyrrhus has suggested that perhaps she did not truly love him (Act IV scene V): *"Je ne t'ai point aimé, cruel ? Qu'ai-je donc fait ?/ [. . .] Ingrat, je doute encor si je ne t'aime pas./ [. . .] Vous ne répondez point ? Perfide, je le vois,/ Tu comptes les moments que tu perds avec moi./ Ton cœur, impatient de revoir ta Troyenne,/ Ne souffre qu'à regret qu'un autre t'entretienne."* [Not love you, dearest? What else have I done?/ [. . .] Ingrate, alas! I think I love you still./ [. . .] Still no reply? Ah villain I see clear/ Each moment spent with me you count too dear!/ Impatient to return to your loved Trojan,/ You cannot bear another's company].

Beckett once again compares Corneille and Racine. For him, Corneille's plays require "doing some work [on the part of the lover] to obtain *l'objet* [of his passion]. Old chivalrous type of sentiment". While in Racine, the "object [is] not even aware of [his or her] lover!" Unlike Corneille, Racine did not use perfect love other than to oppose it to a darker theme – always the principle of antagonisms. The love of Aricie and Hippolyte, in *Phèdre*, for example, is not central to the plot and only serves as a counterpoint to Phèdre's fatal jealousy. These considerations enable

Beckett to move on to *Bérénice*, which he describes as a Racinian tragedy with a Cornelian moral. Bérénice loves Titus and is loved by him. At first glance, it does not seem as if there can be any possible antagonisms. Beckett finds that their relationship is "coldly stated" because "Racine [is] not interested". However, the moral and political obligation that must be faced by Titus, recently crowned emperor, prevents their union: "Opposition [between] duty and love", notes Rachel Burrows. (83)

Beckett tells his students that Corneille and Racine each wrote their version of the story of Bérénice and Titus, that it was "a contest" (later he uses the word "competition") organised by Henrietta of England, sister-in-law of Louis XIV, and that it was Racine's version which enjoyed the greatest success, "beat[ing] Corneille on his own ground". He thinks that, in fact, "[it is the] only play of Racine in which [the] love interest [is] subordinate to [the] political – most unracinian". He finds that there is only one interesting character in *Bérénice*, that of Antiochus. There are some similarities between Antiochus and Oreste, but Beckett thinks that "something of Oreste [is] *perdu* [lost]". (83)

In Beckett's view, Racine "reduces every statement [made by his characters] into [a] cerebral position". He allows us to see what is going on inside their minds. The very essence of *Andromaque* is to be found, Beckett suggests, in Oreste's declaration: "*Je ne sais de tout temps quelle injuste puissance/ Laisse le crime en paix, et poursuit l'innocence./ De quelque part sur moi que je tourne les yeux,/ Je ne vois que malheurs qui condamnent les dieux./ Méritons leur courroux, justifions leur haine,/ Et que le fruit du crime en précède la peine*". [I know not why some dark divinity/Forgets the guilty, hunts the innocent./However I may look upon myself,/I see woes only that condemn the gods./Let me deserve their anger, earn their hate,/And let crime's fruit precede its punishment]. (Act III, Scene I) And Beckett adds that Racine "returns to [the same] statement all through his works". The essence of *Athalie*, on the other hand, is a gesture of piety, but "not for *les jeunes filles*". Beckett suggests that Athalie "is of the stuff of Andromaque, Hermione, [and] Phèdre, [one of the] Racinian heroines".[65] (85)

Bérénice, Beckett reminds his students, is "considered as a comedy of Racine". He goes on to explain that the difference between a Racinian comedy and a Racinian tragedy is in the ending: in the former, it is based on the "establishment of an equilibrium", and in the latter, on the "absolution of any need of equilibrium – finality of divine justice, no longer plurality: no need of equilibrium". For Beckett, *Andromaque*, in which plurality disappears (murder of Pyrrhus, Hermione's suicide, Oreste's madness), is the epitome of tragedy, whereas the dénouement of *Bérénice*, where plurality remains, is balanced by the protagonist's propensity for tolerance. Beckett sees it as a portrait of a "tolerant, sophisticated woman". Her last line, according to him, suggests that she accepts her terrible fate, which is to leave and renounce Titus, "aware of [the] miserable quality of Titus, of the fact that it is a polite *convenance* – not like Corneille's *Bérénice* fanfare of trumpets". (87). Conversely, the least interesting character, in Beckett's view, is Titus, vested with the melodramatic quality that is more suited to Corneille. (88)

In the margin, Rachel Burrows notes Beckett's summary: "Comic spirit: oscillation between equilibrium and lack of it (Molière). Tragic spirit: progression from complexity to integrity". (88)

Beckett also underlines what it is that makes *Bérénice* a "benign comedy": Antiochus does not have the complexity of an Oreste, he is "almost grotesque", "makes grand gesture and suddenly realises it's no good: Bérénice won't take advantage of it [her long speech to Antiochus and Titus]. The 'Hélas !' of

Antiochus at [the] end". (89) Beckett considers the "final complexity" of Antiochus, the character "divided between hope and despair throughout the play", as modern because: "He is denied [a] final lucidity". (88) According to Beckett, for the characters that achieve it, "inner lucidity" is not the result of "control or criticism, [but] simply [a] progressive awareness". (91)

Another aspect of Racine's modernity: Beckett suggests that, in Racine, the "state of mind can't be concealed". In the margin, Rachel Burrows writes "subconscious, modern". (91) This time, Beckett takes the example of *Britannicus* and the "scene where Nero is behind a curtain", during an encounter between Britannicus and Junie: "Nero advises Junie to be standoffish with Britannicus. Britannicus points out that it's no use. Her face will reveal [her] love". In *Bajazet*, on the subject of conflicting feelings, Beckett observes "involuntary betrayal [of emotions] by features. [. . .] Whenever Bajazet sees Roxane, [he] gives himself away." Similarly, in Andromaque: "Pyrrhus gives himself away to Hermione ([in the] scene where he tries to explain things, [he] can't even concentrate)". And Beckett concludes: the "whole victimised organism [is] out of control". (91)

End of the notes on Racine: *"Essay on Oreste"* (in her interview, Rachel Burrows confirms that the words on this page are Beckett's, not her own). For the ex-student, this page is testimony to Beckett's talent as a teacher: "People would say he couldn't teach, but he even got down to the nitty-gritty of showing us how to write an essay on the lesson, with proper headings".

This is what can be read in the notes:

"1. *Développement racinien* [Racinian development] [first part which Beckett describes as 'customary']

2. e.g.: Hermione

3. *Complexité finale d'Oreste* [Oreste's final complexity]
4. Pessimism (*"Je ne sais . . ."*) [I know not why . . .]
5. *Modernité psychologique* (inaccessible mind, stays complex, can't be analysed)." (93)

Rachel Burrows adds in the margin re points 4 and 5 "implications of complexity".

Beckett advises his students to begin their essays with a sentence along the lines of: *"Le pitoyable Oreste, en tant que Racine le sépare du mouvement de clairvoyance progressive auquel il soumet la plupart de ses personnages, répond aux exigences de la psychologie moderne"*. [As a character, the pitiable Oreste fulfils the expectations of modern psychology in that Racine excludes him from the process of increasing perceptiveness to which most of his characters are subjected]. (93) Beckett considers that the first sentence of an essay should not be decorative and must contain all the arguments that will be developed: *"Not flower value but foot-pounds"*, he tells his students.[66] And he adds "Work!" This image exemplifies what he is seeking to impart to them. The introduction must not be merely a beautiful sentence lacking deeper meaning; it must contain all the arguments that will be developed. (92)

For him, the chief argument must be based on the "peculiarity of Oreste", the fact that ultimately he preserves his complexity, that he does not attain integrity. For Beckett, Oreste "stands out". He takes as examples Bajazet and Roxane who have the "Racinian attributes", and contends that Racine has his "habits of characterisation" and that these "recur all the time". (92) Oreste is "one of the few Racinian characters who never reaches one of the polarized sides [of love or hatred]. He ends up in [a]complete lack of orientation", explains Rachel Burrows in the interview. QED.

In 1956, Beckett re-read all of Racine's tragedies. He felt that he approached them with "more understanding of the chances of the theatre today".[67] Twenty-five years after having analysed them with his students at Trinity College, he found that they enabled him to focus his mind on the possibilities of the monologue and on what can be achieved with almost-immobile characters inhabiting a closed world where little, even nothing, changes. Knowlson maintains that this concentrated re-reading of Racine made Beckett reconsider the three fundamental driving forces of drama – time, space and speech, and that this set him on the road first to *Happy Days*, and then on to that of the short monologues of the 1970s.

Harold Pinter recalls that in 1961, on meeting Beckett, for the first time, he got "the distinct impression that he was so involved with his own vision that he had little time and little desire, to read contemporary literature. Beckett preferred to talk of classical drama, particularly Racine, for whom he expressed his never-ending admiration and continuing amazement at being able to find some new interpretation relevant to his own writing each time he read the plays".[68]

CONCLUSION

Beckett also taught Rimbaud, whose works he read constantly, according to Anthony Cronin, and his enthusiasm inspired him to translate *Le Bateau ivre* in 1932, in other words, after having left Trinity College.[69] Other writers Beckett taught or studied reappear in his own writings. According to Deirdre Bair, one of his earliest poems, "Sanies II" (1929, later included in *Echo's Bones*), drew heavily on Valéry and Rimbaud. Beckett found inspiration in *Candide* for a satire, *Che Sciagura* [What a misfortune], which was published in *TCD*, the Trinity College weekly (also in 1929), and in Ronsard, for his short story "Love and Lethe" (published in *More Pricks than Kicks*, Chatto & Windus, London, 1934). A whole catalogue of authors from his degree course emerge in *Proust,* including Anatole France, J. K. Huysmans, Charles Baudelaire and the Goncourt brothers.

Rachel Burrows believes that Beckett's tastes were already clearly formed by the time she knew him, and that "what is so interesting about him is what he liked then and the things that he writes now. [. . .] I can see in this little notebook the germ of what Beckett became, that's why it's so exciting". Knowlson claims that: "However richly innovative much of his later writing was to be, Beckett always saw himself as belonging to and drawing from a wide European literary tradition."[70]

Beckett tried to write, unsuccessfully, while teaching at Trinity College. The "paralysis" he suffered was due to the responsibility of being a teacher. He later explained, on different occasions, that he could not bear teaching others what he did not know himself. The notes we have just examined demonstrate Beckett's modesty. We now know that his approach to literature was erudite, subtle and original. On re-reading her notes, Rachel Burrows was delighted to have been able to act as scribe and to be able to correct Beckett's negative impression of his teaching: "But in fact, he was told to give these lectures, and he conscientiously gave them, and he was really trying to interpret these people for us, which he succeeded in doing. I wish, when you see him, you'd tell him I have always had a great sadness in my heart that this brilliant man, Sam Beckett, still thinks he was a bad lecturer. And I'm the only person I suppose that can correct that image".

We are indeed indebted to Rachel Burrows for having kept this valuable document and for making it available to all those who are interested in Beckett, one of the most extraordinary literary figures of the 20th century. She has thus made the impossible possible: the young Beckett's voice has reached us, giving us an insight into a previously unexplored side of a great artist's development. It is thanks to her that we have today a new perspective on the artistic genesis of Samuel Beckett.

NOTES

1 Trans. note: To teach is to reveal oneself.

2 *Damned to Fame*, p.55.

3 These personal notebooks can be consulted in the Manuscript Room of Trinity College library, Dublin. As far as his French studies are concerned, in addition to Rabelais, they include the French Revolution, Frédéric Mistral (and also mention of the Provençal poets Joseph Roumanille and Théodore Aubanel), and reflections on colloquial language in poetry. The undergraduate teaching syllabus (The Dublin University Calendar) is also available in the same room.

4 *Damned to Fame*, p.48.

5 He mentions her in his very first novel, *Dream of Fair to Middling Women*, p.135.

6 Undated interview with Lawrence Harvey (cf. *Damned to Fame*, p.49).

7 "*Un de mes élèves les plus intelligents, grand ennemi de l'impérialisme, du patriotisme, de toutes les Églises, Sam Beckett, se trouve en ce moment à l'École Normal(e) Supérieure 45 rue d'Ulm, comme Lecteur d'anglais. Il voudrait beaucoup faire votre connaissance.*" Roger Little, "Beckett's Mentor, Rudmose-Brown: Sketch for a Portrait", p.37. According to Little, this letter of introduction does not seem to have helped Beckett. He only met Larbaud through Joyce (Larbaud was his translator), ten years later.

8 According to Henri Debraye's book which Beckett bought in Dublin and on which he based his itinerary, *En Touraine and sur*

the bords de la Loire, Editions J. Rey, Grenoble, 1926. Knowlson notes that Eoin O'Brien now owns this copy signed "S. B. Beckett. Tours August 1926".

9   Translation Knowlson, *Damned to Fame* p.121

10 The document still exists and is available at the Beckett Foundation at Reading University. It is also reproduced in *Disjecta*.

11 "*Ni correspondance ni témoignage, ni biographie ni critique littéraire, l'essai se démarque ainsi, volontairement et immédiatement, des principaux courants de la critique proustienne de son temps.*" *Beckett avant Beckett*, p.79.

12 Bair, p.108.

13 "Dante . . . Bruno. Vico.. Joyce", in *Disjecta*, p.27.

14 Anthony Cronin, p.142

15 Letter from Aileen Conan to Deirdre Bair, 8 August 1972 (Bair p.122).

16 From S. E. Gontarski, Martha Fehsenfeld and Dougald McMillan, "Interview with Rachel Burrows".

17 Letter of 19 June 1973 (Bair, p.123).

18 "Si Balzac avait rédigé Madame Bovary, il l'aurait mieux écrit ; il l'aurait doté de plus grands poumons et d'un cœur plus vivant. Les personnages seraient ouverts comme un fleuve qui se déroule." Georges-Paul Collet, *George Moore et la France*, p.105.

19 "L'adaptation au réalisme français restera toujours incomplète chez eux en raison de la nature même du tempérament anglo-saxon ; il persistera toujours un certain désir de romantisme, avec l'idéalisme qu'il comporte, pour donner un rayon d'espoir dans une existence de déceptions, désir que le roman réaliste russe tend à satisfaire davantage. L'Anglais accepte difficilement un monde où règnent le mal et la complète désolation." Mary Neale, *Flaubert en Angleterre*, p.51.

20 "Tu vas donc te remettre à la pioche ? Moi aussi . . . Que ferons-nous ? Toi, à coup sûr, tu vas faire de la désolation, et moi de la consolation. Je ne sais à quoi tiennent nos destinées. Tu les regardes passer, tu les critiques, tu t'abstiens littérairement de

les apprécier. Tu te bornes à les peindre en cachant ton sentiment personnel avec grand soin, par système. Pourtant on le voit bien à travers ton récit et tu rends plus tristes les gens qui te lisent. Moi, je voudrais les rendre moins malheureux." English translation The Project Gutenberg EBook of The George Sand-Gustave Flaubert Letters. Translated by A.L. McKensie.

21 From now on, page references to R. Burrows' manuscript are given in brackets.

22 This essay was published in *The Egoist*, I, 14 (July 15, 1914).

23 Samuel Beckett, *Dream of Fair to Middling Women, op. cit.,* p.119–20. This novel, published posthumously, has never been translated into French.

24 Gustave Flaubert, *Bouvard and Pécuchet*, trans. A. J. Krailsheimer, Penguin Modern Classics, 1976, p.133.

25 Letter of 8 February 1935.

26 Letter of 14 February 1935.

27 Anthony Cronin, p.202.

28 *Damned to Fame*, p.361.

29 There are three rather than two elements in this analysis of Stendhal's style, which Beckett confirms when he says "the Stendhalian triangle never meets". (97)

30 Beckett, examining the notion of habit in *A la recherche du temps perdu [Remembrance of Things Past]*, picked up on the idea of "living dangerously" and suggested that the Gideans interpreted it as being "the national anthem of the true ego exiled in habit" (*Proust*, p.20). See also *The Faber Companion to Samuel Beckett*, p.227.

31 André Gide, *Dostoevsky* with introductory notes by Arnold Bennett; new introduction by Albert J. Guerard, Greenwood Press, Westport Conn., 1975.

32 Gide cites Dostoevsky's correspondence, "I am conscious that, as a writer, I have many defects, because I am the first to be dissatisfied with my own efforts" and adds "How remote from Balzac with his self-assurance . . .", p.27. Further on, he sums up the great master thus: "Conservative, but not hide-bound by

tradition; monarchist, but of democratic opinions; Christian, but not a Roman Catholic: liberal but not a progressive, Dostoevsky remains ever the man of whom *there is no way to make use!*" p.42.

33 Gide actually says "often irresponsible nature of his characters". This passage describes "The principle charge brought against Dostoevsky in the name of our Western-European logic", p.14.

34 Cf. p.21 in Rachel Burrows' notes and p.72–73 in Gide's essay.

35 Cf. p.21 in Rachel Burrows' notes and p.50 in Gide's essay.

36 It is uncertain whether it is the teacher or the student who shortened the original passage which is: "By reason of this sacrifice and renunciation the most discordant elements are able to live side by side in Dostoevsky's soul, and the extraordinary wealth of antagonism is preserved" (p.23 in the notes and p.71–72 in the essay).

37 "Blessed are the poor in spirit, for theirs is the Kingdom of Heaven." (Mathew 5:3)

38 In fact Gide mentions Saint Paul in connection with the Catholics and contends that, far from Rome, while effectively citing Saint John, Dostoevsky advocates a sort of Buddhism, of Quietism. And it is true that Gide also sees possible comparisons with Stendhal (p.185 et p.187).

39 *Ibid.*, p.142. In her notes, Rachel Burrows has simply written: "*cf. tableau et panorama*. First composition; second bird-eye view. Europeans: *objets éclairés de même façon – point d'ombre*. Cf. Dost. & Rembrandt: importance of shadow, light not diffused [. . .] but from one point . . . Dost. groups persons and events under [a] light which comes from one side. Composition, groups, as picture." (27)

40 Cf. p.29 in Rachel Burrows' notes and p.142–143 in Gide's essay.

41 *Ibid.*, p.145. Rachel Burrows notes: "*Dost. s'intéresse aux abîmes de ses personnages, aux abîmes les plus insondables.*" [Dost. is interested in his characters' gulfs, in the most unfathomable gulfs]. Cf. instinctive French desire for organisation. "*Je ne me charge pas d'expliquer cette coexistence des sentiments contraires*" [I do not take it upon myself to explain this coexistence of conflicting feelings.] (29)

42 On this subject, see John Pilling, "Beckett's Stendhal: 'Nimrod of Novelists'".

43 *Proust*, p.87.

44 ". . . in a foul translation," he states. "Even so it must be very carelessly, badly written in the Russian, full of clichés and journalese: but the movement, the transitions . . . No one moves about like Dostoevsky . . . No one even caught the insanity of dialogue like he did", letter of 29 May 1932.

45 André Gide, *The Counterfeiters*, Translated by Dorothy Bussy, 1931, Penguin Modern Classics, p.166–167. These citations from *The Counterfeiters* are in French in Rachel Burrows' notes.

46 *Ibid* p.168.

47 *Ibid*. p.168.

48 *Ibid* p.169.

49 *Ibid*. p.168.

50 In his correspondence with MacGreevy, Beckett writes he is afraid of starting anything on Gide, even though he has all the necessary notes (31 ? August 1932) and speaks of desperate and vain efforts (13 September 1932).

51 Cf. Bair, p.214. See also Beckett's letters to MacGreevy of January 1931. They reveal that he liked the title of *Voyage au bout de la nuit*, and that he and Pelorson had discussed *Les Conquérants*.

52 *Damned to Fame*, p.49.

53 "We cannot know and we cannot be known" could also be applied to the impossibility of acquiring any knowledge at all absolutely, a theme which is present in Beckett's work.

54 Racine, *Berenice*, Preface, Translated by Samuel Solomon, Random House, New York, 1967. My emphasis.

55 Vivian Mercier, "The Uneventful Event'" *The Irish Times*, 18 February 1956.

56 Cf. the excellent analysis of the relationship between Racine and Beckett by Vivian Mercier, *Beckett/Beckett*, p.75–87.

57 Dostoevsky, p.103.

58 S. E. Gontarski, Martha Fehsenfeld and Dougald McMillan, *Interview with Rachel Burrows*.

59 Cf. Knowlson, p.125.

60 Written in 1947, this play was published posthumously by Les Editions de Minuit, in 1995.

61 *Beckett/Beckett*, p.74.

62 Racine, *Andromache*, Translated by Samuel Solomon, Random House, New York, 1967.

63 Racine, *Phaedra*, Preface, Translated by Samuel Solomon, Random House, New York, 1967.

64 Beckett seems here to persist in thinking that she is not entirely indifferent to Pyrrhus.

65 Then he moves on fairly briefly to *Britannicus*, "une très belle pièce" [a beautiful play], but the notes are too succinct and quite difficult to decipher to attempt to relay them here. The notes of another of Beckett's students at the time, Grace West, do not yield much more (see *Beckett Remembering / Remembering Beckett*, p.311).

66 The choice of words gives a glimpse of the burgeoning writer.

67 Letter to Thomas MacGreevy, 4 June 1956.

68 According to a conversation with Deirdre Bair in 1974 (see p.445).

69 This translation, edited by James Knowlson and Felix Leakey, was published under the title *Drunken Boat* by Whiteknights Press (Reading, England) in 1976.

70 *Damned to Fame*, p.55.

BIBLIOGRAPHY

Notes taken by Rachel Burrows née Dobbin of the lectures of Samuel Beckett on Gide and Racine. Michaelmas 1931 [Library of Trinity College, Dublin, MIC 60].

Samuel Beckett, *Malone meurt*, Les Editions de Minuit, 1951
_____, *Dream of Fair to Middling Women*, edited by Eoin O'Brien and Edith Fournier, Arcade Publishing, 1992
_____, *Disjecta, Miscellaneous Writings and a Dramatic Fragment*. Edited with a foreword by Ruby Cohn, John Calder, 1983
_____, *Proust and Three Dialogues* (with Georges Duthuit), Calder & Boyars, 1965
_____, *Correspondance avec Thomas MacGreevy*, 1930–1967, unpublished
C. J. Ackerley & S. E. Gontarski (eds.), *The Faber Companion to Samuel Beckett, A Reader's Guide to His Works, Life and Thoughts*, Grove Press, 2004
Deirdre Bair, *Samuel Beckett*, Jonathan Cape, 1978.
Ruby Cohn, *A Beckett Canon*, University of Michigan Press, 2001
Georges-Paul Collet, *George Moore et la France*, Librairie Minard, 1957
Anthony Cronin, *Samuel Beckett, The Last Modernist*, Flamingo, 1996

Jean-Pierre Ferrini, *Dante et Beckett*, Hermann, 2003

Gustave Flaubert, *Bouvard et Pécuchet*, Paris: GF-Flammarion, 1966

Gustave Flaubert–George Sand: Correspondance, Flammarion, 1981

André Gide, *Dostoevsky* with introductory notes by Arnold Bennett; new introduction by Albert J. Guerard, Greenwood Press, Westport Conn., 1975

S. E. Gontarski, Martha Fehsenfeld, and Dougald McMillan, *Interview with Rachel Burrows*, Dublin, Bloomsday, 1982, in *Journal of Beckett Studies*, Nos. 11 & 12, 1989, p.6–15. Also available at http://english.fsu.edu/jobs/num1112/006_BURROWS.PDF

Lois Gordon, *The World of Samuel Beckett 1906–1946*, Yale University Press, 1996

Charles Juliet, *Rencontre avec Samuel Beckett*, Fata Morgana, "Explorations", 1986

James Knowlson, *Damned to Fame. The Life of Samuel Beckett*, Bloomsbury, 1996.

James & Elizabeth Knowlson (eds.), *Beckett Remembering / Remembering Beckett, Uncollected Interviews with Samuel Beckett & Memories of Those Who Knew Him*, Bloomsbury, 2006

Roger Little, "Beckett's Mentor, Rudmose-Brown: Sketch for a Portrait", *The Irish University Review*, Vol.14, No.1, Spring 1984, p.34–41

Vivian Mercier, *Beckett/Beckett*, Oxford University Press, 1977

Seán O'Faoláin, "The Irish Conscience?", *The Bell*, vol. XIII, No.3, Dec. 1946, p.67–71

Mary Neale, *Flaubert en Angleterre, Etude sur les lecteurs anglais de Flaubert*, SOBODI, 1966, p.51.

John Pilling, *Beckett before Godot*, 1997

_____, "Beckett's Stendhal: 'Nimrod of Novelists'", *French Studies* L (3), 1996 p.311–316

Jean-Michel Rabaté, *Beckett avant Beckett. Essais sur les premières œuvres*, "Accents", PENS, 1984

Nicholas Zurbrugg, *Beckett and Proust*, Colin Smythe, 1988